Modeling the Market:

New Theories and Techniques

Sergio Focardi
Caroline Jonas

Published by Frank J. Fabozzi Associates

Copyright © 1997 by Frank J. Fabozzi
New Hope, Pennsylvania

ISBN: 1-883249-12-0

Printed in the United States of America

1 2 3 4 5 6 7 8 9 0

TABLE OF CONTENTS

ABOUT THE AUTHORS

Sergio Focardi is a partner of The Intertek Group. Before forming The Intertek Group, he was a director of Control Data. Dr. Focardi has authored and coauthored numerous articles, reports, and books on simulation and adaptive methods in research and industry. He holds a degree in Electronics Engineering from the University of Genoa and has a specialization in Communications from the Electrotechnical Institute Galileo Ferraris in Turin.

Caroline Jonas is a partner of The Intertek Group. Before forming The Intertek Group with Sergio Focardi, she was a senior consultant, Europe, with Regis McKenna Inc. Ms. Jonas has coauthored reports on advanced computational methods in banking and finance. She holds a B.A. in Political Science from the University of Illinois, Urbana-Champaign.

The Intertek Group is a Paris-based consultancy specializing in technical and scientific computing in banking and finance. It undertakes research and training on the use of advanced computational methods in the financial services sector.

PREFACE

Together, the availability of high-performance computing and high-frequency data have unveiled *stylized facts* relative to financial phenomena that are hard to explain within today's finance theory. The explanation of these facts is, however, of relevance to investment and risk management. Efforts to explain recent empirical discoveries attempt to capture the learning and decision-making processes of agents as well as the non-equilibrium behavior of the market.

These efforts are often associated with forecasting and market efficiency, but the debate on forecasting and market efficiency is perhaps misplaced. Market efficiency is a robust idealization given the present conceptual framework of theoretical finance. It constrains but does not preclude forecasting.

From a theoretical as well as a practical standpoint, the issue is *how well* models perform. To improve over present performance, new concepts — different from the rational stochastic representation of finance — will be required and are in the making. The concepts of market efficiency and equilibrium will, perhaps, have to be redefined.

Adaptive computational methods are proving to be important tools. They have improved our ability to represent, forecast, and select basic risk factors. In addition, the technology of optimization has gained a much broader scope, enabling problem-solving methodologies that are proving highly beneficial.

Based on interviews with over 100 persons in industry and academia, *Modeling the Market: New Theories and Techniques* provides a framework for understanding recent parallel developments in finance theory and financial modeling, and their practical applications. The first three parts of the book present key ideas in the making and describe a new generation of computer-based applications, discuss technical and management issues, and outline the development of the financial software market. The last part offers a technical overview of relevant concepts.

ACKNOWLEDGMENTS

This book is based on interviews with over 100 persons from banking and finance, the research community, government, hardware, software, and service suppliers, and outside observers in the United States and Europe, conducted in 1995.

The authors wish to thank the persons and organizations listed below, who contributed to this book by sharing with us their experience and their views.

Financial institutions in the U.S.: Atlantic Portfolio Analytics & Management, Chase Manhattan Bank, Citibank, Countrywide Funding, Fidelity Investments, First Quadrant, Lehman Brothers, Merrill Lynch, Morgan Stanley, Prudential Securities, SBC Warburg.

Financial institutions in Europe: ABN-Amro, Allianz Life Insurance, Banca Commerciale Italiana, Bank Sal. Oppenheim Jr., Barclays Bank, Chemical Bank London, Credit Lyonnais, ING Bank, James Capel, Kredietbank, Morgan Grenfell Asset Management, Schroder Investment Management, TSB Bank, Union Bank of Switzerland (UBS), SBC Warburg.

Researchers in the U.S.: W.B. Arthur (Santa Fe Institute), T. Bollerslev (Northwestern), S.V. Coggenshall (Los Alamos National Laboratory), B. LeBaron (University of Wisconsin), M. Makivic (Syracuse University), M.T. Melvin (Arizona State University), J. Moody (Oregon Graduate Institute), M. O'Hara (Cornell), S. Srivastava (Carnegie Mellon), S. Zenios (Wharton

School of Economics).

Researchers in Europe: D.-E. Baestaens (Erasmus University-Rotterdam), P. Embrechts and D. Wuertz (Swiss Federal Institute of Technology-Zurich), K. Frauendorfer (University of St. Gallen, CH), C.A.E. Goodhart (London School of Economics), S. Goonatilake (University College London), A.N. Refenes (London Business School).

Software and service companies: Algorithmics, BARRA, C*ATS, Foundation Technologies, IBM Scientific Center-Paris, Infinity, Intelligent Financial Systems, Neural Trading Systems, NeuralWare, Neurotec, Nonlinear Prediction Systems, Olsen & Associates, The Prediction Company, Quantum Development, Reuters NewsMedia, SearchSpace, Strategic Economic Decisions, Tica Technologies.

Hardware suppliers: Cray Research, IBM, Siemens-Nixdorf.

Government: the Commission of the European Community, the German Federal Ministry for Research & Technology, the U.K. Department of Trade and Industry.

Outside observers: *The Economist*, *Financial Times*, *Handelsblatt*, *Risk*, *Wall Street & Technology*.

N.B.: Some persons may have changed position since we talked to them. Reference is made to persons in function of the post they occupied at the time of the interviewing.

PART I
CONCEPTS AND METHODS

1. BASIC CONCEPTS

1.1 The classical view of finance

Classical finance theory is based on the assumption that financial markets are made up of skilled participants that share similar information and act rationally and without delay to new fundamental information that might signal a profit opportunity. Traders quickly exploit such opportunities. By doing so, they create excess demand for profitable securities whose prices are thereby readjusted. As a consequence, trading occurs in conditions near equilibrium. The idealization of the above is the Efficient Market Hypothesis (EMH).

Classical finance theory translates the notion of perfect markets into mathematical conditions that constrain the evolution of security prices. As there is always uncertainty in finance, finance theory is cast in the framework of the theory of probability. Uncertainty is represented by admitting a number of different states of the economy and by assuming that a probability structure can be imposed on the set of states.

Formally, classical finance theory is built around three key concepts: no arbitrage, agent optimality, and equilibrium. Market participants or agents are represented as maximizers of utility functions defined over the set of possible states. The condition of no arbitrage can be stated as the impossibility of making a risk-free profit without any investment. The condition of equilibrium means that agents reach independently their condition of optimality without leaving any residual unsatisfied demand or sup-

1

ply; the sum of trades is zero. Agents are assumed to know the probability structure of the economy. In equilibrium, there is a perfect balance between agents' decisions and the evolution of the economy.

The above conditions are not independent. In particular, the condition of no arbitrage is equivalent to the solvability of the agent optimality problem. Intuitively, this means that there is a trade-off between different portfolios, allowing an agent to determine the optimal portfolio in function of his or her risk/return schedule. Were there arbitrage, on the other hand, it would be possible to make arbitrary gains through leverage.

Classical finance theory is embodied in a number of probabilistic self-consistent models that respect the conditions of no arbitrage, agent optimality, and equilibrium. It demonstrates that these models are mathematically possible, proves a number of very general relationships, and studies the representation and the properties of each model. It does not, however, state how investors effectively evaluate information and produce rational expectations.

It is possible to look at market efficiency from the point of view of each security using the martingale concept. A martingale is a stochastic process, i.e., a sequence of random variables so that at every moment their expected value at any future instant is equal to their present value. The simplest example of a martingale is a random walk, such as the cumulative sums of heads and tails obtained by flipping a fair coin. At every flipping, there is a 50% chance that the coin will come up heads or tails. This implies that after every flipping the expected value of the cumulative heads and tails is the present value.

Following concepts introduced in 1976 by Eugene Fama of the University of Chicago, the efficient market hypothesis is generally stated in terms of the statistical concept of martingales. Security prices do not, however, follow martingales. The price of a stock, for instance, typically has an expected positive return. This difficulty could be easily overcome in a risk-neutral world by taking the sum of future gains discounted at the risk-free rate. Fama's initial definition of market efficiency through the notion of martingales was effectively valid in this condition only.

In general, however, future gains need to be discounted not at the risk-free rate but at a risk-adjusted rate. Determining the latter is not trivial. It can be shown that the hypothesis of no arbitrage is equivalent to the existence of an *equivalent martingale measure* for the discounted gain process. In other words, the actual expected values of discounted gains do not follow a martingale, but it is possible to define an equivalent probability measure under which they do.

The equivalent martingale measure condition does not imply that security returns are not forecastable, but puts constraints on their forecastability. It in fact imposes constraints, albeit weak ones, on the risk/return relationship of each security. It requires that there is only one risk-free rate; any forecast of return different from the risk-free return must show uncertainty. The actual risk/return characteristics of the market remain unspecified.

The efficient market hypothesis is deeply rooted in the theory and the practice of finance. Charles Goodhart, the Norman Sosnow professor of banking and finance at the London School of Economics, remarks that the EMH is a strong hypothesis and serves as a fundamental frame of reference. The market, he notes, is quite efficient. Many interviewees, academics and practitioners alike, remarked that the market is comfortable with the classical vision as a frame of reference and is generally satisfied with the modeling that it generates.

The efficient market hypothesis is not a single compelling hypothesis, but a full-fledged global theory. It does not describe the actual structure of the market but states that the evolution of financial quantities can be approximated by some equilibrium, no-arbitrage model. In fact, there are a potentially infinite number of models compatible with the EMH. It is possible to adjust models to fit empirical data with increasing accuracy. This makes it difficult to conclusively prove or disprove the EMH. Using non-stationary processes and a variety of different statistical tools, research has extended the scope of the EMH well beyond the limits of its initial crude characterizations.

1.2 The new paradigm of empirical finance

Although made flexible by sophisticated mathematical tools, the classical vision of finance remains a "rational" conception of a possible economy only approximately in agreement with actual data. The availability of data, due mainly to the diffusion of electronic transactions, is behind the development of a more empirically based theory of finance. Tim Bollerslev, the Nathan S. & Mary P. Sharp distinguished professor of finance at the J.L. Kellogg Graduate School of Management at Northwestern University, remarks that the field of finance has been driven by the uncovering of "stylized facts," i.e., statistical findings on the behavior of financial time series. The availability of high-frequency data will, he believes, affect our understanding of issues such as the microstructure and efficiency of the market. Prof. Bollerslev maintains that the market must now be looked at in a dynamic state.

The new theorization posits that markets are made up of heterogeneous participants or agents. Participants do not share the same time horizons. These span a variety of time periods, from the short periods of speculators to the long periods of the central banks. Different time horizons produce internal delays in implementing decisions, resulting in non-equilibrium situations. Participants do not have the same risk profile or motivation for trading.

A large amount of trading is due to the need to fulfil commitments made in the past or to other non-speculative motives. Trading decisions vary from trader to trader, even when they share the same expectations. But market participants neither share the same knowledge, nor have the same perception. As a result, markets have an inner structure and show patterns of response to external events. These patterns are statistically predictable.

One consequence of the above is that the relationship between risk and return implied by the classical theory of dynamic asset pricing no longer holds. This is due to the fact that differences in returns are not only a function of risk but also of non-equilibrium forces. Market participants do not make perfect all-encompassing evaluations of risk and return, but act on imperfect knowledge and under constraints. Although investor behavior might still be modeled by utility functions, in a real-world framework the maximization of the expected utility is a dynamic process that must take into account realistic expectations and constraints.

The above considerations point to the possibility of studying financial markets as autonomous processes that respond to external events. Market behavior is examined using large amounts of past data, such as high-frequency bid-ask quotes of currencies or stock prices. It is the abundance of data that makes possible the empirical study of the market. Although it is not possible to run controlled experiments, it is possible to extensively test models on historical data.

Statistical analysis has accumulated a wealth of stylized facts about economic and financial time series that cannot be easily explained by classical theory. Empirical studies of financial time series have shown that the distribution of returns deviates from the predictions based on classical theory. In a series of papers, Michel Dacorogna, Richard Olsen, and co-researchers at Olsen &

Associates have explored how foreign exchange markets respond to external inputs. Their findings demonstrate that the foreign exchange markets do not react immediately to new inputs, but show patterns of response that can be forecast. They point out that the huge amount of trading in foreign exchange is due largely to market participants that have different time horizons, creating a chain of trades to fulfil obligations. Different time horizons impose constraints, creating an internal structure in the market.

The work of Zurich-based Olsen & Associates demonstrates that foreign exchange markets have structure that can be revealed through experimental and theoretical analysis. It is important to note the experimental basis of the work: it shows relationships between theoretically defined variables tested over large samples of data, as in an engineering process.

From the point of view of the global functioning of the economy, there is a new theoretical approach that views the economy as a complex system far from a state of equilibrium. Small initial changes might produce large changes, as processes are highly non-linear. These effects are not simply small local deviations from a state of equilibrium, but imply that the economy follows complex non-linear laws. The next chapter outlines how these ideas translate into theories and models.

1.3 A new theory in the making

Findings from the empirical study of the economy have not yet been consolidated into a theoretical formulation as comprehensive and coherent as that offered by classical theory. There are theoretical obstacles to a new theory. While classical theory models the decision-making process of agents as utility maximization in a situation of equilibrium, a non-equilibrium theory must face upfront the challenge of modeling how agents make decisions based on the information available to them. This implies modeling the intelligence, logical reasoning, learning capabilities, and motivation of agents.

In addition, the modeling of intelligent behavior must be coupled with an ensemble view of the economy that takes into account phenomena related to the complexity of the system. The study of complexity has revealed that in complex systems fluctuations in the interactions between agents are not necessarily averaged away. Small events, such as single decisions, might have enormous consequences.

Northwestern University's Tim Bollerslev remarks that it is difficult to foresee if researchers can come up with an explanation of the many new facts that have been discovered in the statistical modeling of financial time series. It is impossible to point out one single hypothesis that needs to be rectified, as theories respond to observations in a global sense. Prof. Bollerslev believes, however, that the newly discovered facts will not affect our fundamental understanding of basic financial processes such as asset pricing.

The availability of large quantities of historical data suggests the use of a data-rich approach to improve econometric models. The modeling of non-equilibrium effects is largely obtained through adaptive methods that create models by adjusting parameters in a generalized mathematical structure. In so doing, adaptive methods provide modeling capabilities without the need, upfront, of an all-encompassing theory. In addition to statistical modeling, neural networks and genetic algorithms are perhaps the most widely used of the adaptive tools.

Most new theoretical results are, in fact, statistical analyses of time series. Researchers have developed statistical models of the behavior of empirical time series that show a good level of agreement with observations. The ARCH and GARCH families of models — developed by Robert Engle and Tim Bollerslev, respectively — have shown the ability to model the time evolution of volatilities of many processes. However, no existing general econometric model provides a faithful dynamic, non-equilibrium description of large portions of the economy.

Adaptive computational methods reconstruct local phenomena on a statistical basis. They do not provide a theory. Many persons interviewed for this book were skeptical, to various degrees, of the ability to develop adaptive methods into a full-fledged axiomatic theory. An axiomatic theory is a conceptual framework where available knowledge is embodied in a small number of statements from which all facts and laws can be derived by logical deduction. Most physical sciences are cast in an axiomatic form. The classical theory of finance is also an axiomatic theory.

Are the new adaptive methods now being developed one step towards the formulation of a formal global theory? What is the relationship between the statistical description of time series and a possible unified theory of the market based on an understanding of the structure of information flows and the decision-making process of agents?

Maureen O'Hara, the Robert W. Purcell professor of management at Cornell University's Johnson Graduate School of Management, remarks that there is always a natural tension between time series analysis and structural models. Time series analysis attempts to improve over structural models, but she considers it to have the basic limitations of an *ad hoc* solution. Prof. Bollerslev concurs. He remarks that a deeper theoretical understanding is needed, as a purely adaptive approach does not, he believes, allow much progress in the long run.

Charles Goodhart of the London School of Economics remarks that the impossibility of conducting controlled experiments stands in the way of empirical finance developing into an axiomatic framework. Prof. Goodhart cites the need for a better understanding of how market operators change their opinions, the interaction between rational agents, including how they interpret each other's behavior, and the effects produced on different agents with different objectives and different time horizons. Rational agents learn from the price changes of other agents.

Blake LeBaron, associate professor of economics at the University of Wisconsin-Madison and a co-developer of the Santa Fe Institute's computer simulation of a virtual stock market, notes that new models of how people learn and adjust are required. He believes that the empirical study of the economy is now ahead of theoretical studies, and that the theories that the former requires are different from the classical theories. Prof. LeBaron underlines the need to understand microstructure issues in order to measure the impact of news on market participants and the mechanics of how traders trade. He also cites the need to understand the learning process from the point of view of how prices are set, taking into consideration that market participants are not fully informed agents. A behavioral approach should, he believes, be complemented by a learning approach, as each stresses different aspects of economic theory that should be weakened.

A learning approach, which implies a strong attack on the efficient market hypothesis, comes from the field of complexity studies. At the Santa Fe Institute, a team of academics led by W. Brian Arthur and including Prof. LeBaron have shown how to simulate a market of intelligent traders, using notions of genetic evolution. Prof. Arthur rejects the notion that the economy is in a state of equilibrium and that market participants all form the same rational expectations. He points out that economies are complex dynamic systems characterized by instabilities that generate growing returns. Investors, he maintains, do not share the same information, nor do they arrive at the same conclusions, because each has his or her own internal model.

As head of the economic program at the Santa Fe Institute, Prof. Arthur leads a project to simulate the functioning of markets by making intelligent agents interact. Agents develop their own models of the economy, and make their own forecasts. Their decisions are influenced by how they think other agents will react. Although still highly idealized, this is a global model of the economy that takes into consideration the exchange of information between market participants and the strategizing related to individual perceptions. The Santa Fe Institute model has shown the ability to reproduce a number of important features of real markets.

Following on the work of Stanford University's Mordecai Kurz, Horace W. Brock, president and founder of Strategic Economic Decisions in Menlo Park, California, is an advocate of market inefficiencies. Dr. Brock maintains that market participants do not share a single rational belief, but that each participant has a set of beliefs that are rational related to his or her own position. This hypothesis implies that there is structure in the market, and thus forecastability. However, Dr. Brock believes that forecastability cannot be captured by statistics but rather by a sound theoretical formulation of non-equilibrium economics. This, he believes, is now within reach thanks to the ground laid by Prof. Kurz. Dr. Brock points out that there are structural changes in the economy that modify the specific form any economic model might have. Markets can be forecasted, he maintains, only by deducting from a theoretical framework the causal relationships between economic variables.

There are attempts to combine a data-rich approach with econometric modeling. At Carnegie Mellon University, Sanjay Srivastava, professor of economics and finance, has launched a research program to build general econometric models using non-linear forecasting methodologies. Econometric models are generally built using a large set of linear relationships that contain free parameters to be optimized. Prof. Srivastava is using machine-learning techniques to build a new generation of more powerful econometric models.

To summarize, the fundamental advance of present research in financial and economic theory is to replace the hypotheses of general equilibrium and market efficiency with a more realistic hypothesis of how markets work. This more realistic hypothesis will be based on experimental data. In the new formulation, the dynamic behavior of markets will no longer be characterized as "anomalies," but as consequences of the intrinsic structure of the market. Dr. Olsen likens the present state of economic theory to that of physics at the beginning of the century, when accumulated experimental evidence had made it clear that a conceptual breakthrough over classical physics was needed. There is yet no complete, mathematically sound dynamic theory of the economy, but partial theories of some of the components do exist. In addition, a technology for forecasting has been developed, making it possible to capture some of the practical benefits of market dynamics.

The following paragraphs explore a number of concepts important to financial modeling and, in particular, to the new concepts of empirical finance.

1.4 Probability and beliefs

From a scientific point of view, finance would be a rather dull subject were it not for the uncertainty and risk associated with present decisions whose consequences carry forward in time. It is the management of uncertainty that has propelled finance into the realm of quantitative science.

The conceptual handling of uncertainty and the ensuing computational methods are presently based on the theory of probability. Probability is a full-fledged mathematical theory developed as an axiomatic system. The theory makes a number of assumptions and develops consequences logically. Its interpretation and its applicability to the description of phenomena is, however, a factual empirical question.

A number of interviewees underlined the need to attain a high level of sophistication in the understanding of statistics and probability. Inderjit Sandhu, senior consultant at Barclays Bank in London, prescribes a thorough mastery of statistics for anyone working in adaptive methods. Suran Goonatilake, a researcher in computer science at University College London, remarks that a strong statistical basis is necessary to make adaptive methods robust enough for industrial use.

Although the probabilistic framework is conceptually and mathematically well-known, the application of probability in finance is problematic. The usual meaning of probability in science is related to the consideration of a large number of identical entities. When we say, for instance, that there is a certain probability that an individual will develop a specified disease, we mean that the proportion of people that actually develop that disease in appropriately selected samples is close to the number that we take as probability. There are many subtleties in this concept but, basically, probability means the relative frequency of an event.

In a number of financial applications, however, this concept is difficult to apply, as there is only one realization of the relevant time series. What do we mean when we say that there is a certain probability that a currency rate will go up tomorrow? How can we verify if our statement is correct? We cannot count, tomorrow, the relative frequency of the specific currency rate that actually went up, because there is only one rate. Experimental evidence is limited to the past values of rates. Eventually their future values could be taken into consideration. To give experimental meaning to the notion of probability, it is necessary to look at past and future cases, linking probabilities to relative frequency with respect to time.

In most financial applications, probability statements can be verified only by inferring time distributions and time statistics. This implies taking an abstract view of probability and assuming rules to translate probabilities into time statistics. The simplest and most stringent assumption is that probabilities do not change over time and that probability averages are close to time averages. In general, it's necessary to assume that distributions change with time and, thus, to develop a complete dynamic theoretical framework that relates probabilities to measurable quantities, i.e., past and future values of time series.

Probability has another meaning, namely individual judgment on the likelihood of some future event. This is to be intended as a statement that an entity makes at a given moment regarding future events. Although it implies judgment, it is not a psychological concept: a machine could make this type of judgment. The notion of the degree of likelihood of a judgment is a concept difficult to define. Still, judging the likelihood of events is what most people do daily in business. Most decisions are based not on statistical evaluations, but on chains of reasoning about the likelihood of future events.

In finance theory, there is sometimes confusion between a statistical and a judgmental view of probability. This confusion can create difficulties. These difficulties are made more severe by the fact that, as remarked above, probability distributions are assumed, as abstract hypotheses, to be verified indirectly through time statistics. It should be clear, however, that it is necessary to distinguish between 1) probability distributions as hypotheses to explain the actual processes, i.e., the behavior of financial quantities, and 2) probability distributions as determinants of the decision-making processes of market participants.

Probability theory might not be the best mathematical ideal-ization of the decision-making process under uncertainty. In many instances, we are uncertain in ways that are poorly repre-sented by probability measurements. As finance begins research into the microstructure of the market, a more faithful modeling of the uncertainty related to investors' decision-making processes might be needed. This is a difficult and largely unexplored field.

A number of academics and practitioners have explored the consequences of using representations of informational ambigui-ty. The University of Toronto's Larry Epstein and Tan Wang amended the standard inter-temporal asset pricing model, allow-ing for information ambiguity. Umberto Cherubini, head of the forecasting and risk management research unit at the Milan-based Banca Commerciale Italiana, applied non-additive utility to modeling the loan renegotiation process between a bank and a firm under distress. In another area, Dr. Cherubini used a para-metric representation of information ambiguity through a special class of parametric fuzzy measures to model investors' behavior under uncertainty. These concepts were then applied to the pric-ing of corporate debt.

These efforts represent an innovative approach to the prob-lem of understanding the relationship between intelligent agents. This problem has high priority in the present academic research agenda. Many feel the need to go beyond the classic paradigm of utility maximization. Concepts of information ambiguity and non-additive utility developed by the artificial intelligence and decision sciences communities might well prove to be a key con-ceptual advance in the analysis of market microstructure.

A related subject is that of behavioral economics, i.e., how people react to news and judgements. Maureen O'Hara, professor of management and finance at Cornell University, questions whether real-world decision rules are indeed those that we have been pursuing. Individuals in the aggregate might, however, be more rational than as single units; Prof. O'Hara does not exclude this possibility. The University of Wisconsin's Blake LeBaron remarks that, given observations that show that people react in ways different from what prevailing theory predicts, the "optimizing agent" paradigm might have to be modified. Prof. LeBaron believes that a behavioral approach should be part of the explanation of the decision-making process.

The above underlines that the consideration of the decision-making process of market participants raises difficult modeling questions. A combination of artificial intelligence concepts and economic theory is required.

1.5 Modelability of financial laws

To many, modeling finance is difficult or impossible, as it is believed that the laws themselves change with time. Others note that financial laws change on observation, as the knowledge gained influences investors' decision-making processes. Still others believe that no law can be truly representative of reality. These are difficult objections, because they deal with the problem of what a law is. To make the question meaningful, one has to specify the type of laws admitted. The point is that there are different levels of laws in function of what they describe and different types of mathematical relationships to describe the laws. Highly general models represent high-level relationships between variables that might involve a significant level of conceptualization. To make models informative, it is necessary to sacrifice generality to capture local features.

Models built using adaptive methods are represented by relatively simple mathematical functions containing a number of parameters. They are created with a training procedure and used over a period of time. They might lose accuracy and need retraining. If the interval of validity is too short, phenomena are not modelable with functions represented by simple functional forms learned by adaptive procedures. In practice, the question of modelability with adaptive procedures is a question of whether a chosen set of parameters is valid for a sufficiently long period and, eventually, how to detect when to implement changes.

To reach a higher level of generality, there are two basic strategies. One is to assemble different models of a lower level that might be suitable for different regions of the data. The question is how to decide what model to use and when, and if decisions involve human judgment or can be made automatically. The second strategy is to reach for a higher-level, all-encompassing description. The latter generally implies some conceptualization that goes beyond pure data.

The problem of modelability was raised often during field research, showing some convergence of opinion but no general agreement. Norman Packard, co-founder of The Prediction Company, believes that financial time series are modelable and that, if properly designed, models are stable for a long period. The Prediction Company uses sophisticated models made of an assembly of more elementary models. Advanced stacking techniques that combine a set of lower-level models are used for adopting the model best suited to each region of the data. Dr. Packard remarks that an event as important as the Gulf War did not produce significant disruption in their models. He does, however, say that over long periods of time models must be modified.

Dr. Packard's views are shared by others who believe that automated procedures can make the switch between different models adapted to different regions. ABN-Amro Bank has identified three markets, the trading market, the trending market, and the changing market. A trading market is one that moves in a narrow range with a solid bottom and a heavy barrier; a trending market moves up or down; and a changing market goes from trading to trending or vice versa. According to Bob Emanuels, technical analyst at the Amsterdam bank, they are now working on nonlinear methods to improve the indicators that determine the automatic switching from one model to another.

Others, though maintaining that financial time series are modelable, believe that there are changes in the economy that modify the functional relationships between parameters in ways that cannot be automatically predicted. Suran Goonatilake, researcher at the University College London computer science department, believes that whatever modeling approach is taken, it will be valid only for a limited amount of time: machine-learning procedures cannot handle the constant shocks to the system.

One solution can be to combine machine learning with judgmental procedures. Dr. Goonatilake believes that it is possible to get closer to an automatic forecasting system using hybrid techniques that combine genetic algorithms with expert rules. He believes, however, that turbulent situations will require a human expert. This opinion is shared by other researchers and practitioners who believe that sound theoretical judgment should be used to understand if something new is happening. Morgan Stanley's Charles Marshall, vice president for fixed-income research, attributes management's prudent attitude towards machine learning to the fear of market glitches not detectable by adaptive methods.

Other researchers question whether some financial time series are modelable at all with adaptive methods. According to Paul Refenes, senior research fellow at the London Business School, understanding if a series is stable enough to allow for profitable training is a big question. Dr. Refenes believes that there might effectively be markets that change too rapidly to be modeled with adaptive techniques. ABN-Amro's Bob Emanuels thinks that there will always be markets that remain unmodelable.

Researchers such as Michel Dacorogna and Richard Olsen, who believe in a strong theoretical description of market behavior, also believe that conceptual thinking is necessary. To arrive at a general theory of the foreign exchange markets, research at Olsen & Associates was conducted in three steps: first, an analysis of seasonalities; second, a change in the time coordinate; and third, the consideration of autocorrelations. These steps, they claim, could not have been made by machine-learning procedures, as they imply fundamental scientific creativity.

1.6 Chaos theory

The existence of a descriptive mathematical model of a process does not imply that actual values of the variables describing the process can be computed. There are differential equations, even simple ones, that cannot be numerically integrated with any level of precision. Other mathematical conditions cannot be translated in computational terms at all. The existence of a mathematical model is a theoretically strong condition that might have no practical meaning.

These considerations lead us to the much debated subject of chaos theory and its applicability to financial phenomena. Chaos is a concept that lends itself to misconceptions. An interesting review of the theory is provided by E. Atlee Jackson in his paper *Chaos Concepts*.

Although the first intuition of chaos is due to the French mathematician Poincaré, the modern development of non-linear dynamics started with the observation — made by MIT meteorologist Edward Lorenz — that numerical solutions of a particular differential equation produced diverging results for changes in the initial parameters due to rounding-off errors. Subsequent studies have shown that solutions to a vast class of non-linear differential equations might diverge, even if they come arbitrarily close to each other. In other words, there are solutions that are arbitrarily close at a certain point but diverge thereafter.

If, however, solutions are plotted in the state space and some special sections are taken, intersections cluster around patterns called attractors. Non-linear differential equations might have solutions that are non-periodic but cross in arbitrarily closed points and show definite statistical properties. These properties were found in simple differential equations and in simple numerical mappings. This type of mathematical behavior is called chaotic determinism.

The fact that simple equations are capable of very complex behavior created the hope that the complexity of economic phenomena could be explained as chaotic determinism. There are additional theoretical considerations to be made, but we would like first to point out the intrinsic difficulties in applying chaos to any physical phenomenon. Fundamental scientific laws are thought to be a faithful description of nature within the limits of experimental accuracy. When aggregates are considered, they are measured as accurately as is technically possible. If probabilities are used, as in quantum mechanics, it is supposed that distributions are verified as relative frequencies within the limits of attainable precision. Even minor discrepancies need to be explained and might cause a major theoretical revision.

Chaos is a different type of explanation. When a physical law is said to be of a chaotic type, this means two things. First, the mathematical law describes the underlying physical process only locally. Second, on a large scale, the statistical behavior of the physical phenomena is the same as that of the mathematical law. For instance, weather forecasts based on present models are valid only for a few hours; the same models are used to study the statistical behavior of weather over long periods of time. It is never-theless possible to maintain that the path actually followed by a chaotic system is approximated by a set of the possible paths described by mathematical equations. There is, however, no way to associate a specific mathematical solution with a specific physical path.

Chaotic behavior as it occurs in the physical sciences has this twofold characteristic of models based on simple differential equations that show both local validity and large-scale regulari-ties as attractors. It is this duality of behavior that researchers are trying to exploit in finance by inferring local forecastability from the emergence of large-scale regularities typical of chaos. The assumption of theorists is that, if complex behavior is organized around attractors, it is likely that local behavior can be explained through simple systems.

Field research showed a diversity of opinions on the applica-bility of chaos theory to financial forecasting. For researchers like Norman Packard, among the founders of the theory, chaos provides a wealth of concepts and techniques. The algorithms he and co-researchers at The Prediction Company use were original-ly developed in their study of the mathematics of chaos theory. Dr. Packard would, however, be very careful in answering ques-tions such as "Is the market chaotic?"

Others remark that chaos theory is too demanding in terms of data to be of practical utility. Georges Darbellay, who holds a doctorate in physics from Oxford University, and is now in charge of computational methods for trading at the Union Bank of Switzerland, believes that the application of the fundamental the-orems of chaos theory would require amounts of filtered data that might well exceed all currently available data. In a paper present-ed at the First International Conference on High-Frequency Data in Finance (Zurich, 1995), Dr. Darbellay and fellow researchers used time-delay embedding to forecast currency and interest rates. Their results demonstrate that there is little evidence of chaos in currency and interest rate time series.

Most interviewees simply feel that chaos theory is conceptually too complex to find much application in finance today. Many, however, recognize that chaos theory played an important role in spreading the notion that financial markets can be scientifically understood. Dirk-Emma Baestaens, from the department of finance at Erasmus University-Rotterdam, says that chaos theory was useful in convincing even the most die-hard conventional econometricians that there is forecastability in financial markets. Dr. Refenes observes that there is growing agreement that price data move according to deterministic and random components but that the random component is on its way to becoming a minor component. Dr. Goonatilake adds that chaos has a role in defining the broad characteristics of the market.

1.7 Fractals

Fractals have commanded a high level of interest in the financial community. The notion of fractals was put forward in the 1960s by Benoit Mandelbrot, a mathematician working at the IBM research center in Yorktown Heights, New York. Mandelbrot observed that many naturally occurring phenomena have descriptions that depend on the scale of the measurements and that these descriptions are often self-replicating. He observed, for instance, that there are scaling laws in the distribution of commodity prices over different periods.

Mandelbrot invented fractals as mathematical structures that describe geometric self similarity and was able to identify a number of properties of self-similar structures. The public knows of fractals through the beautiful color images that can be produced by fractal algorithms. More seriously, fractal mathematics has become an important mathematical tool.

Fractals have strong intellectual appeal. They translate the notion of scale — important to every sector of science — into rigorous mathematics. Behind every simplifying hypothesis, and thus behind every theory, is the underlying belief that phenomena can be described with a certain level of complexity up to a certain scale and that additional levels of complexity happen only below that scale. Although this might seem a trivial statement, it is a fundamental hypothesis of physical laws. When violated, major scientific revisions become necessary.

Fractals go deeper into the scaling laws by establishing fundamental self-similarity that translates the appealing notion of a natural template that repeats itself. Over the last three decades, self-similarity has permeated the world of science, particularly physics. Chaos theory has made use of concepts derived from fractals by showing that some chaotic patterns — known as attractors — are fractal objects.

The application of fractal theory to finance has, however, proved to be more difficult and technically demanding than originally expected. London Business School's Paul Refenes remarks that fractals are a particularly complex way of implementing chaos theory. The major contribution of fractal theory to finance has been the finding of rather deep scaling laws that connect statistical parameters. These ideas were popularized by Edgar Peters of PanAgora Asset Management in his book *Fractal Market Analysis*. Peters developed the fractal market hypothesis (FMH) as an alternative to the efficient market hypothesis. The FMH is expressed through scaling laws that are assumed to govern the market.

Scaling laws have been found in many financial time series. Researchers at Olsen & Associates have shown that the volatility of foreign exchange rates follows a scaling law when computed over different periods. This scaling law shows structure in exchange rates; their evolution is quite far from a random walk.

1.8 Forecasting

The notion of forecasting seems intuitively clear but turns out to be complex. To appreciate the difficulties, consider the following. There are time series generated by computer algorithms that behave as statistical "white noise," i.e., completely random, uncorrelated variables. Commercially available algorithms, called random number generators, can produce such sequences of numbers. Although generated by purely deterministic procedures, they pass every practical test for randomness.

Forecasting can be cast in a probabilistic framework: it is the knowledge of the conditional probability distribution of a random variable at a future time given the information presently available. If the conditional probability distribution of a certain variable at a future time given the present state is known, it is possible to make forecasts whose accuracy depends on the shape of the distribution itself. If the probability distribution is flat, there is no information and thus no forecastability; each future value is as likely as any other. At the other extreme, if the probability distribution is highly concentrated in a certain point, we have near perfect knowledge. For any distribution in between, forecasting will involve an amount of uncertainty.

How to define a quantitative measure of forecastability given a known stochastic process is a theoretical problem that is complementary to the problem of measuring risk. Measurement of forecastability becomes meaningful within a specific probability framework. From a conceptual point of view, forecastability can be considered an intrinsic characteristic of a stochastic process. Given the probabilistic description of a stochastic process, its forecastability is derived from the probability distribution of its random variables.

From the point of view of the forecaster, however, forecastability entails the ability to produce a forecasting model. In practice, one is presented with a time series whose probability distributions are unknown. The problem of forecasting is to determine a possible stochastic process that generates the empirical data with acceptable precision. A time series is forecastable if there exists a generating process able to generate future values with an information-carrying statistical distribution. Theoretically deterministic series might appear random, while apparently forecastable series might hold unpleasant surprises.

It should be noted that measures of uncertainty in time series forecasting have a different meaning than measures of risk in the classical paradigm. Forecasting introduces uncertainties related to forecasting models whose performance is not theoretically determined. While classical risk is a statistical uncertainty that the market can supposedly evaluate precisely, forecasting risk is related to the performance of an algorithm. This point has proved to be crucial in management's evaluation of forecasting methods.

The notion of forecasting has come to be associated with the new dynamic non-equilibrium framework, opposing forecastability to the intrinsic randomness of efficient markets. This is, however, somewhat misleading. The classical theory of the economy does not preclude the forecasting of financial quantities: rational agents "know" expected values of securities and their future probability distributions. Efficient markets are forecastable but there are upper bounds to forecastability. These are prescribed by the risk/return relationship implied by asset pricing models. An efficient market implements optimal forecasting that translates into the market price.

The point that forecasting and the efficient market hypothesis do not necessarily contradict each other was made by Aamir Sheikh, formerly assistant professor of finance at Indiana University and now manager of derivatives research at the financial software company BARRA (Berkeley, California). Dr. Sheikh observes that there is a lot of forecasting going on within the framework of the EMH. He cites as examples the forecasting of returns and volatility in portfolio models. In this context, forecasting is essentially an exercise in parameter estimation within an equilibrium framework.

The paradigm of finance now in the making differs from the classical one in not imposing theoretical restrictions on forecasting. More precisely, no theoretical restriction has yet been proposed, as we still lack a non-equilibrium asset pricing theory for heterogeneous markets. The new framework states that the market is neither optimal nor efficient. It should thus be possible to find patterns. Forecasting becomes theoretically profitable.

It should, however, be remarked that there is no true arbitrage opportunity, even in a non-equilibrium framework. Arbitrage implies that arbitrary gains can be made. Forecasts entail a level of uncertainty, and there is a trade-off between the perceived opportunity for returns and the uncertainty associated with the forecast. Revealing potentially profitable relationships in security prices is not sufficient to ensure profit; the associated uncertainties have to be taken into account.

Academics interviewed remarked that forecasting is, by nature, a difficult exercise. Prof. Goodhart of the London School of Economics observes that markets are close to efficiency and that any small edge that can be found risks being whittled away. From the point of view of the academic community, forecasting is not generally considered a major research goal. The interest of the academic researchers centers on questions of market structure and efficiency. Academics need stationarity, the University of

Wisconsin's Blake LeBaron says, and forecasting patterns change. He adds that while the amount of forecastability that can be pulled out of the market is not sufficient to allow an academic researcher to claim finding an important, significant structure, it may be sufficient to make a trader quite happy.

Most of the forecasting effort today is, therefore, being carried out by industrial researchers. Academics interviewed generally feel that even a small edge, e.g., being right on directional forecasts 51% of the time, can justify the large industrial investment that a number of companies are making. Michael Melvin, professor of economics at Arizona State University, says that there *is* evidence of short-term profitability in the foreign exchange markets due to the use of forecasting. He doubts, however, that the exercise will prove profitable in the long term.

John Moody, associate professor of computer science at the Oregon Graduate Institute, considers forecasting technologies a moving target. He believes that their use might have reduced profitability in the less liquid markets where there is a high level of deployment of these technologies. Prof. Moody nevertheless expects the use of forecasting technologies to increase substantially and identifies as a major challenge the ability to capture and integrate fundamentals.

1.9 The notion of risk

Risk exists because there is uncertainty about the future course of events. One can make a forecast about the future and accept, at a certain price, the risk of deviation from the expected values. As risk deals with uncertainty, the natural theoretical framework for understanding risk is probability. The complete risk profile of a security is expressed by the probability distribution of its returns. Using the same concept, one can define the risk profile of a market sector as the probability distribution of some index. This notion is subject to the same considerations already made for forecasting. There are conceptual difficulties in applying probability notions to time series that have only one realization, as probabilities can be estimated only through past realizations.

Risk is essentially the possibility that realized values differ from expected values, or that they fall outside a certain expected interval. If the probability distribution of a financial time series is known, it is possible to compute the risk associated with the series, computing the expected value of the series and the probability that actual values fall within a specified interval. From a theoretical standpoint, a thorough understanding of risk implies the knowledge of all the joint and conditional probability distributions making up a complete financial model.

Knowledge of distribution functions is, however, generally beyond reach. To manage risk, simplifying assumptions are made, in particular, assumptions that allow the characterization of risk with a single variable. One measure of risk that is usually taken is the standard deviation of the distribution. As there is only one time series for each security, standard deviation is measured by the deviation of past values of the series.

Risk is a theoretically defined concept. The ability to measure risk with some variable depends on the ability to construct a full-fledged theory around the notion of risk. In other words, it depends on the possibility of establishing functional relationships between measures of risk and other quantities. There is no quantity that can be considered a "natural" measure of risk in and of itself.

Understanding and quantifying risk is a complex matter. Karl Frauendorfer, professor of operations research at the University of St. Gallen (Switzerland), cites the need to compute more faithful distributions over a fixed time horizon to improve on our evaluation of risk. Tim Bollerslev, professor of finance at Northwestern University, expects that high-frequency data will help to better characterize the distribution of returns, leading to better risk scenarios.

1.10 From financial analytics to empirical finance

The following chapters trace the technological path from the classical rational vision of economy to new empirical approaches as they are now developing and being put into practice. The continuity in the technological approach to finance should be underlined. Although the notions of empirical finance based on high-frequency data are truly a conceptual revolution, in practice there is a continuous path of applications from the existing methodologies and tools to the new adaptive ones. There are three major levels in this path or evolution of the technology of computational finance.

i) Level 1: state-of-the-art financial analytics.

State-of-the-art financial analytics is based on the handling of uncertainty in the framework of general-equilibrium no-arbitrage models of the economy, using the mathematical tools of continuous-time stochastic processes.

Continuous stochastic modeling under general-equilibrium assumptions is state-of-the-art computational finance at most firms. This technology has reached maturity and is now being used in trading and risk management. Chapter 2 describes current technology as offered by major suppliers and applied by financial firms.

ii) Level 2: technological developments within the classical framework.

Among the technological developments within the framework of state-of-the-art financial analytics are the handling of compound transactions, large-scale optimization techniques, high-performance computing for real-time evaluations, tools for financial engineering, user-friendly man-machine interfaces including the intelligent presentation of results, software engineering methods for managing the growing costs and complexity of applications, and automatic news analysis.

At financial firms and suppliers of financial software alike, there is a lively research and development effort going on within the classical framework. Some of this development makes use of adaptive non-linear methods such as genetic algorithms and neural networks. Chapter 3 covers major lines of development.

iii) Level 3: a data-rich approach to studying financial phenomena and new economic theories.

The new approach to economics and finance is based on relaxing the general-equilibrium no-arbitrage assumptions and embracing the scientific handling of the dynamics of financial processes, using forecasting methods and/or dynamic macroeconomic theories. The two lines of development here are a data-rich approach to economic and financial phenomena and new economic theories.

Chapter 4 deals with technological developments based on a new theoretical framework, including the dynamic non-equilibrium modeling of financial phenomena using high-frequency data. From a practical point of view, most of the commercial development effort is going into forecasting volatilities, prices, and returns given the potential reward of the exercise. The availability of high-frequency data is encouraging academic researchers to build an empirical understanding of financial phenomena with the ultimate goal of creating a comprehensive finance theory. Chapter 4 covers some of the major lines of research.

References

Arthur, W.B., "On the Evolution of Complexity," *The Santa Fe Institute Paper*, No. 93-11-070, 1993.

Bernstein, P.L., *Capital Ideas. The Improbable Origins of Modern Wall Street*, The Free Press, New York, 1992.

Bollerslev, T., "Generalized Autoregressive Conditional Heteroskedasticity," *Journal of Econometrics*, 31: 307-327, 1986.

Brock, H.W., Hsieh and B. LeBaron, *Nonlinear Dynamics, Chaos and Instability*, MIT Press, 1991.

Goodhart, C.A.E. and M. O'Hara, "Introductory Lecture: High Frequency Data in Financial Markets, Issues and Applications," *First International Conference on High-Frequency Data in Finance*, Zurich, 29-31 March 1995.

Jackson, E.A., "Chaos Concepts," *1992 Lectures in Complex Systems*, Lecture Vol. V, Santa Fe Institute Studies in the Sciences of Complexity, Editors L. Nadel and D.L. Stein, Addison-Wesley, Reading, MA, 1993.

LeBaron, B., "Forecast Improvements Using a Volatility Index," *Journal of Applied Econometrics*, 7: S137-S150, 1992.

O'Hara, M., *Market Microstructure Theory*, Blackwell Publishers, Cambridge, MA, 1995.

2. MODELING UNDER EQUILIBRIUM

2.1 Financial modeling today

The last decade witnessed the development of financial modeling techniques. Major Wall Street firms hired hundreds of physicists, mathematicians, and engineers to design and build financial models. Initially, development was done in secrecy and gave a competitive edge. Applications are now marching towards maturity and have, to some extent, reached standardization. Off-the-shelf financial analytics packages are available.

Although the actual use of quantitative models varies from firm to firm, it is fair to say that financial modeling has changed the practice of finance. The impact of modeling on finance is defined by David Leinweber, managing director at the Pasadena, California-based investment management firm First Quadrant, when he says the company's business is "using computers and mathematics to make money for people."

Classical equilibrium modeling is the explicit technological choice of most firms. Andrew Morton, a co-developer of the HJM model of the term structure of interest rates and now head of modeling for fixed-income derivatives at Lehman Brothers, remarks that the firm's conception of the market adheres to the EMH. Their objective, he says, is sound modeling, not betting against the market. Most Wall Street firms interviewed for this book would concur.

Ultimately, financial modeling must produce forecasts of the future evolution of securities, because forecasts of risk and return are the fundamental information on which investment and trading decisions are based. Classical models make their forecasts under the constraints of the EMH. The hypothesis of market efficiency and of no arbitrage substantially reduces the set of independent risk factors by establishing links between different securities. Only a small number of risk factors need to be forecast, while the entire market behavior can be derived from first principles.

The principles of asset pricing will be explored, followed by a discussion of the four basic building blocks in classical financial modeling:

- forecasting the return and risk profiles of stocks,
- pricing derivative securities,
- forecasting the term structure of interest rates, and
- implementing optimal decision-making.

2.2 Asset pricing models

Classical financial modeling is based on selecting some statistical model for the behavior of a security's price and deriving mathematical conditions that constrain the evolution of security prices and returns. A number of different assumptions on the evolution of prices and returns, all consistent with the no-arbitrage and equilibrium conditions, can be made. Investors choose those models that best reflect empirical data and their risk and investment management needs.

The most basic model considers the behavior of securities over a fixed time horizon. In this case, the model is simply the probability distribution of returns at the end of the period. Models are characterized by different hypotheses about the shape of probability distributions and utility functions. Single-period models are mathematically tractable and offer a simple and intuitive representation.

Under the assumption of no arbitrage and additional reasonable assumptions on probability distributions, it can be shown that the probabilistic behavior of the entire market can be expressed in function of a small number of independent risk factors. The Capital Asset Pricing Model (CAPM) of Sharpe-Lintner-Mossin considers only one risk factor, the *beta* factor. The *beta* factor represents the covariance of a security or a portfolio, with the "market portfolio" defined as a portfolio that includes all possible investments in the proportion in which they actually exist. Other models, such as the multifactor CAPM and the Arbitrage Pricing Theory (APT), consider a number of different factors for generating the returns of each stock in a portfolio.

These models consider only a single period. It might, however, be important to consider the behavior of security prices over multiple periods. The basic methodology remains the same, but there is the additional complication of defining a probability structure that reflects changes over time.

It is assumed that the economy can be in a number of different states. The set S of states represents all the possible outcomes of the economy over the $T+1$ periods considered, from $t=0$ to $t=T$. As usual in probability theory, a probability structure is imposed on the set of outcomes by associating a probability to each event. An event is a set of possible outcomes.

Probabilities are defined over families of events F that are closed under the operation of complement and union. These families are called algebras of events. The standard representation of the time evolution of probabilities makes use of the concept of *filtration*. Filtration represents how information is revealed through time. It associates to each period t a subalgebra $G(t)$ of events so that $G(t)$ includes events that can be ascertained true at time t. This probability structure is the basic framework for defining the distribution of probabilities of returns at each instant as well as all the conditional probability distributions.

In the multiperiod setting, most results of the single-period setting still hold, but their formal expression is more complex. In particular, there is no simple relationship between present prices and future returns, because in a multiperiod setting the present prices depend on the risk/return profile for each period. It can be shown that the no-arbitrage condition is equivalent to the existence of an equivalent martingale measure for the cumulative discounted gains. This is an important result, as it allows one to perform computations in a risk-neutral equivalent world. The multiperiod setting allows for the same simplification of the single-period setting because, under appropriate assumptions, all the returns can be computed from basic risk factors.

The above models are discrete models that consider only a finite number of trading periods. An important innovation in finance was the introduction of continuous-time mathematics. This was achieved by assuming that there are an infinite number of traders and that trading is continuous in time. This is a truly mathematical idealization, as continuous trading is a theoretical limit of actual trading situations. The advantage of this approach is the ability to use a vast body of established sophisticated mathematics. In the continuous-time mathematical framework, prices can be represented by diffusion processes. Diffusion processes are used in physics to represent the motion of particles in a fluid, with the particles subject to a large number of small independent shocks.

The random fluctuations around a constant rate of return — a model of returns on stocks — constitute a simple type of diffusion process. In general, however, the evolution of security prices is supposed to follow a more general type of diffusion process known as the Ito process. An Ito process is characterized by an instantaneous rate of return and by an instantaneous volatility. In the language of stochastic differential equations, Ito processes express the conditions that, in every infinitesimal time interval, price changes are made up of a deterministic increment in expected value plus random fluctuations. These random fluctuations are supposed to follow a zero-mean normal distribution independent of the past distribution of values.

The assumption that security prices follow Ito processes is consistent with the EMH. Other types of statistical models of security prices consistent with the EMH are also possible. In particular, it's possible to consider processes with rare "jumps" that correspond to external shocks to the economy.

As one might expect, most results obtained in a multiperiod setting still hold in a continuous-time framework. Their formulation is, however, mathematically more complex and loses the intuitive meaning of the discrete case. However, as we will see below, the adoption of continuous-time mathematics made it possible to establish connections between the prices of basic securities and the prices of derivative securities. In a no-arbitrage framework, the evolution of prices of derivative securities can be derived mathematically from that of basic securities. The process of consolidation has been carried one step further. An investor need not independently forecast derivative prices, but can compute them from the theory.

As remarked by Charles Marshall, vice president for fixed-income research at Morgan Stanley, it is surprising to see how fast the notion of continuous-time finance has permeated the sector. Over the time span of a decade, mathematics has revolutionized finance. Representing the evolution of security prices as Ito processes enabled the present generation of financial models; it provided the sound mathematical basis on which the algorithms have been built.

2.3 Forecasting stock prices and returns
The basic model for forecasting prices and returns of stocks

considers forecasting over a single time horizon. In a no-arbitrage framework, forecasting stock prices and returns is accomplished using a Capital Asset Pricing Model (CAPM). The CAPM is the conceptual foundation of modern portfolio management. It maintains that it is reasonable to assume an idealized market model with a firm relationship between risk and return. Deviations from this situation are considered mispricings. The CAPM also provides the conceptual base for performance evaluation through benchmarks, as it shows that a conveniently chosen benchmark is representative of the results that it is reasonable to expect from investments.

The multifactor implementations of CAPM and/or multifactor APT models express returns as a linear combination of a number of factors. Each factor is a random variable; each security has a random term that expresses that specific security's risk. The risk/return of any portfolio can be determined in function of the composition of the portfolio. Multifactor models are essentially statistical tools for estimating the risk and return of a portfolio under the assumptions of the EMH. They implement the rational expectations of investors in the classical framework. Using a multifactor model, a firm can determine the risk/return profile of every possible portfolio and choose the optimal portfolio using standard optimization techniques.

Industry assessment of CAPM and multifactor models covers a rather broad spectrum of opinions. Multifactor models have been developed in-house by many firms. With $18bn in institutional assets under management, First Quadrant relies on multifactor models for tactical asset allocation. The Pasadena, California firm uses quantitative models to direct timely shifts in major segments of portfolios. First Quadrant builds and refines its models using adaptive genetic methods. A number of software companies also offer multifactor models. BARRA, a commercial developer, offers multifactor models that are now in use at hundreds of sites.

At Morgan Grenfell Asset Management in London, multifactor models such as APT are state-of-the-art. The firm uses BARRA software and has developed its own APT model. David Jessop, a Cambridge-trained mathematician and quantitative fund manager and analyst at the $50bn investment firm, says that multifactor models are used to model market risk, isolating the market component of portfolio risk. He remarks that, although multifactor models are linear and entail simplifications, they are useful.

Another consideration is clients' requirements for a quantitative evaluation of risk. Andrew Simpson, an investment manager at Schroder Investment Management, says that the use of multifactor models is becoming increasingly common, even in low-risk fund management. Clients and consultants, he remarks, want risk quantified and are increasingly using this sort of technology. The London firm has over $90bn in assets under management.

2.4 Derivatives pricing

The pricing of derivatives is a major achievement of classical financial modeling. Computer models calculate the theoretical pricing of derivative products in function of the volatilities of underlying securities. Alternatively, models compute the volatility implied by the actual market price of derivatives, i.e., they evaluate the volatility that would yield the actual price of derivatives. These models are used as decision-support tools for traders or become part of a portfolio management application.

The technology for pricing derivatives follows the seminal work of Fischer Black and Myron Scholes on the pricing of options first published in 1973. In its classical formulation, the pricing of derivatives depends on the assumption that the price of underlying securities follows an Ito process. In a perfect market, and assuming that a security follows an Ito process, it can be shown that options written on the same security likewise follow an Ito process. The idea is to form a portfolio that includes the underlying security and the option in such a proportion as to be instantaneously risk-free. No-arbitrage arguments require that this instantaneously risk-free portfolio earn the risk-free rate. A differential equation that must be satisfied by prices is derived from this condition. Black and Scholes have, in some cases, been able to solve this equation explicitly, producing their celebrated option pricing formula.

Since the publication of Black and Scholes' seminal work (*The Pricing of Options and Corporate Liabilities*), many models have been proposed for the pricing of options and other derivative securities. A major advance was the use of the martingale approach in derivatives pricing. The key was to show that the pricing of derivatives can be accomplished assuming a risk-neutral world. In such a world, all securities earn the risk-free rate of return and a martingale for prices can be constructed. Using these mathematical techniques, pricing formulas and computations are simplified.

A number of numerical methods for computing derivatives prices have been developed. Although in some cases closed-form solutions of the Black-Scholes equation can be found, in general numerical approximation methods are required. There are two major strategies for pricing algorithms. The first solves the differential equations satisfied by prices using standard numerical methods for approximating solutions to differential equations. The second generates a large number of possible paths that satisfy the stochastic equations for the evolution of derivatives prices and computes prices as averages over a large number of possible paths.

The pricing of derivative securities is state-of-the-art modeling at major firms. Models are now available commercially, and research is extending the analysis to more complex products and markets. According to our interviewees, users and suppliers alike are comfortable with these models. Michael Zerbs, vice president for financial engineering at Toronto-based Algorithmics, remarks that derivatives analysis following the Black-Scholes framework is now widely accepted market practice and represents a common frame of reference. Dr. Zerbs believes that market participants know how to adjust for models' shortcomings. Founded by Ron Dembo, a former professor at the management and computer science faculties at Yale, Algorithmics provides pricing, financial, and risk management models.

Given a model for the pricing of derivatives, it is possible to evaluate how prices will change in function of changes in parameters such as volatility and interest rates. These rates of change are given conventional names in the industry: *delta* is the rate of change of the price of a derivative with respect to the price of the underlying asset, *theta* is the rate of change of a portfolio of derivatives with respect to time, *gamma* is the rate of change of *delta* with respect to the price of the underlying security, *vega* is the rate of change with respect to volatility, *rho* is the rate of change with respect to interest rates, and so on.

The above functions are used to design hedging strategies. Starting from the analytical expression of the various rates of change, it is possible to compute the composition of portfolios that are risk-free, leading to hedging techniques. These techniques have, however, a drawback: they create portfolios that are risk-free for only an instant. Keeping a portfolio constantly hedged requires frequent and costly rebalancing.

2.5 Interest rate models

Models of the evolution of interest rates are a fundamental building block in the analysis of fixed-income securities and their derivative instruments. Term structure models provide the basis for the evaluation of securities such as bonds, forward and futures contracts, and swaps, as well as options and other derivatives.

Interest rates are difficult to model as they involve an entire term structure, i.e., the level of interest rates over an entire period as opposed to only a specific moment. A forecast of expected values of interest rates is, however, implicit in the price of financial products such as government bonds, which depend on interest rates. In making a forecast of future interest rates, the present implicit market forecast of interest rates must be taken into account.

Modeling interest rates implies creating a theory on how the entire term structure will evolve over time. The simplest approach assumes that interest rates have a parallel shift, without considering changes in the shape of the term structure. This is clearly a crude approximation, used nevertheless in bond analysis. A more realistic approach models term structures through an Ito process as if they were prices of stocks. However, these models are at odds with empirical findings: interest rates do not assume arbitrary values, but tend to stay close to some long-term value. This is known as mean reversion.

More accurate models of the term structure of interest rates assume that interest rates follow an Ito process but add a "mean-reversion" term which assures that the long-term behavior of interest rates is more in line with empirical data. It has been shown by Cox, Ingersoll, and Ross that models of this type can be derived from a general-equilibrium model of the economy. These models are characterized by stochastic differential equations. An important issue in practical applications is to make models compatible with the present term structure. The initial term structure is then taken as the initial condition for numerical procedures.

2.6 Decision-making under uncertainty
The investment allocation theory is based on the seminal work

of Harry Markowitz on portfolio management. Following Markowitz, investments are allocated by maximizing the expected value of the utility function of each investor, taking into consideration his or her evaluation of probability distribution functions for the price of securities at the end of the investment period. It is a mathematical model of how a rational investor would manage a portfolio of investments. It posits that investors act according to decision rules that model the risk/return trade-off of each investor through the maximization of their expected utility. Risk/return preferences, i.e., utility functions, are considered a given.

The theory of financial decision-making is independent of the theory of asset pricing one might subscribe to. It is a theory of how decisions are made under uncertainty. It can be applied to any process characterized by a probability distribution of values and utility functions. One might reasonably ask how well it represents the real-world decision-making process and whether it has any independent justification.

The key problem in financial decision theory is the lack of objective knowledge, as investors do not have any sure knowledge of probability distributions. They cannot rely on well-tested theories, but can only make rough guesses of probabilities, often from relatively small samples. Often investors are simply uncertain and not able to quantify their uncertainty in mathematically tractable probability distributions. For this reason, research is exploring different paradigms for the handling of uncertainty.

References

Fabozzi, F.J., F. Modigliani and M.G. Ferri, *Foundations of Financial Markets and Institutions*, Prentice Hall, Englewood Cliffs, NJ, 1994.

Jarrow, R.A., *Modelling Fixed Income Securities and Interest Rate Options*, McGraw-Hill, New York, NY, 1996.

3. Technological Developments in the Classical Framework

Within the framework of general-equilibrium no-arbitrage principles, research and development efforts are extending the scope of analysis in the following areas:

- more extensive modeling
- numerical methods
- forecasting and estimation of parameters
- global optimization
- high-performance computing
- financial engineering tools
- intelligent human interfaces
- automatic news analysis
- simulation.

The following paragraphs look at each of these developments separately.

3.1 More extensive modeling

Although financial models are now state-of-the-art, there are many efforts to build more efficient, more comprehensive models. A first line of development concerns asset management. Current multifactor models are one-stage optimization algorithms that consider only one period. At the end of the period, portfolios need to be rebalanced. Intertemporal optimization using Bellman's dynamic programming is rare, given the technique's complexity and computational requirements.

An interesting new approach is stochastic programming. Pioneered by George Dantzig of Stanford University in the mid-1950s, stochastic programming combines probability and optimization theories for analyzing the interaction between decision-making and uncertainty. It has received increasing attention in finance in the U.S. and in Europe. Among researchers applying stochastic programming to finance are Karl Frauendorfer at the University of St. Gallen (Switzerland) and Stavros Zenios at the Wharton School of Economics.

The multistage stochastic optimization approach considers the portfolio optimization problem over several periods, with optimization decisions being made at each stage. The algorithms optimize over the entire multistage period, taking into account the uncertainty at each point.

In the area of derivatives, an important line of development is the evaluation of risk in compound transactions when transactions and their hedging occur in different markets. Although this problem is conceptually similar to that of evaluating transactions in a single market, it is computationally more complex. The development of analytics to handle cross-market transactions was cited as a priority by most large firms. Erik Carlson, director of strategic analytics and research at Prudential Securities, considers the handling of compound transactions a significant extension of the present technology of evaluating, pricing, and managing risk. He adds that, with the increasing globalization of operations, cross-market analysis is an analytical must. These comments might be considered representative of the thinking inside major financial firms.

Advances are also being made in the area of pricing derivative instruments based on interest rates. The pricing of interest rate-based derivatives is different from the pricing of options on stocks: interest rates cannot be characterized by a single volatility parameter, but need the consideration of an entire term structure. The first generation of models for pricing interest rate-based derivatives used a Black-Scholes type of analysis. Clearly an oversimplification, a new generation of models is now being proposed, that describe the evolution of interest rates and are in agreement with the present interest rate term structure.

Among the models proposed, the Heath, Jarrow, and Morton model (HJM model) is the most complete one presently available. A number of firms are developing HJM-type models. A drawback of these models is, however, the computing power required. To solve the problem, less computationally onerous models that nevertheless describe the evolution of interest rates and are in agreement with the present term structure have been proposed. Among them, the model developed by John Hull and Alan White, professors of finance at the University of Toronto, is widely used. The Hull-White model is available as off-the-shelf software from A-J Financial Systems, a company founded by Hull and White.

There is also important research going on to develop models that allow volatility and return rates to be either deterministic functions of both time and security prices or to be stochastic variables themselves. In the latter case, suitable stochastic equations describe the evolution of volatility and return rates. Other models are based on combining a "diffusion process" approach with a "jump" approach that takes into consideration rare external events.

3.2 Numerical methods

An important area of research concerns numerical methods for computing derivatives pricing. Black and Scholes solved the option pricing equation in closed form in some particular cases. Closed-form solutions for derivatives pricing are not, however, generally available. With the diffusion of low-cost high-performance computers, finding closed-form solutions has become less important, because numerical methods for solving differential equations are available. Finite difference methods and Monte Carlo simulations have become commonplace.

New developments are related to the diffusion of parallel systems. Monte Carlo methods are "embarrassingly parallel" algorithms: each computation is independent of the others. Monte Carlo simulations can therefore be run on a parallel machine simply by assigning the computation of different simulation paths to separate processors. These methods might, however, require significant amounts of computing power to obtain a high level of accuracy.

A new approach to Monte Carlo methods — the path-integral Monte Carlo method — was proposed by Miloje Makivic of the Northeast Parallel Architectures Center (NPAC) at Syracuse University. The path-integral Monte Carlo algorithm computes the probability distribution for the complete history of the underlying security. An advantage of this approach is the amount of information that can be obtained from each simulation. In particular, it is possible to compute price sensitivities to all input parameters and prices for multiple parameter values. The path-integral Monte Carlo method can be applied to arbitrary stochastic processes, including jump-diffusion and non-stationary processes, as it uses the Metropolis algorithm to sample underlying histories.

Following a different line of thinking, a new breed of methods for computing derivatives pricing uses neural networks and other approximation algorithms. MIT professors Andrew Lo and Tommaso Poggio have shown that neural networks can learn pricing formulas for derivatives with great accuracy. Their work points to the possibility of training neural networks on either actual market prices, learning the market pricing process, or on theoretical prices derived from computer simulations.

Umberto Cherubini, head of forecasting and risk management research at the Milan-based Banca Commerciale Italiana, and Emilio Barucci and Leonardo Landi of the University of Florence, used neural networks as semi-parametric estimators of the solutions of pricing differential equations. Their work shows that neural networks can approximate solutions of differential equations by analytic methods, without learning from actual solutions. Dr. Cherubini also explored other approximation schemes by considering general functional representations of pricing functions, in particular orthogonal polynomials. The key idea is to assume a representation for the pricing function and then to apply mathematical conditions represented by differential equations.

The interest of these developments is two-fold. On one side, these techniques are numerically efficient, hence their usefulness in complex pricing problems. Implemented on parallel structures, they allow fast pricing algorithms. More important, the combination of learning schemes and mathematical conditions from theoretical analysis allows pricing valuations in closer agreement with empirical data without ever leaving the ground of the no-arbitrage principles that form the conceptual basis of derivatives pricing.

3.3 Forecasting and parameter estimation

The classical framework of finance has come to be associated with an essential randomness of price behavior and the impossibility of outperforming the market with profitable forecasts. Books such as Burton Malkiel's *A Random Walk Down Wall Street* have popularized this theme for private investors.

These notions are, however, somewhat misleading. The efficient market hypothesis (EMH) states that there is a basic efficiency in the market that precludes earning excess profits through trading within the framework of the risk/return decision rules.

Investors can forecast risk and return and optimize their positions, either maximizing returns for an acceptable amount of risk or minimizing risk for acceptable returns. The EMH allows for forecasting, but dictates that it will be subject to firm relationships. Market deviations from the predictions of the EMH are considered as temporary mistakes or mispricings that the market will correct.

The efficient market hypothesis is a set of abstract mathematical conditions that relate quantities such as volatilities and expected returns. These latter need to be estimated and forecast. As remarked by Aamir Sheikh, head of derivatives research at the financial software firm BARRA, there is a lot of forecasting now being done, even within the classical framework. Dr. Sheikh makes a distinction between the forecasting of risk and the forecasting of returns. He believes that forecasting technologies are presently good at forecasting risk, while their ability to forecast returns is much less satisfactory. Berkeley, California-based BARRA uses non-linear techniques, in particular GARCH modeling, for forecasting volatilities in their commercially available portfolio optimization models. GARCH volatility forecasting models are now a standard component of the company's multifactor model.

Karl Frauendorfer, professor of operations research at the University of Saint Gallen in Switzerland, considers forecasting — in the sense of computing probability distributions at a given time horizon — a major goal of research. He believes this is a promising type of forecasting and foresees its application on a large scale.

In the area of derivatives pricing, the use of forecasting models is more problematic. Distinctions, however, have to be made. The classical algorithm for derivatives pricing is based on assumptions about the evolution of the underlying securities.

More realistic assumptions on the behavior of the underlying securities, i.e., better forecasts of their behavior, produce better pricing algorithms. Important innovations in this area are the consideration of time-varying or stochastic returns and volatilities.

Many interesting results have been obtained. Dr. Sheikh, formerly assistant professor of finance at Indiana University and now at BARRA, and the University of New Mexico's Gautam Vora have shown how implied volatilities can be estimated through the Black-Scholes models in the case of stochastic volatilities.

A different application of forecasting techniques implies, however, the rejection of the no-arbitrage framework for derivatives pricing. Derivatives can thus be considered as securities to be independently forecast. At MIT's Sloan School of Management, Andrew Lo and Jiang Wang have found that there are possible correlations between options' prices and the underlying securities' returns; derivatives pricing might depend on the evolution of returns. They have shown that neural networks are able to learn the derivative pricing algorithm and to learn from the time series of actual market prices.

The industry, however, remains somewhat skeptical about forecasting. Michael Zerbs, vice president of financial engineering at Algorithmics, believes that the performance of forecasting algorithms today is insufficient to justify a major effort to include forecasting in their pricing models.

3.4 Global optimization

Optimization is ubiquitous in financial applications. It is a key component of portfolio management systems and risk management procedures. It is also a fundamental building block in financial engineering. Optimization procedures such as mathematical programming have been in use for several decades.

There are presently a number of important advances. One problem in optimization is dealing with multiple optima. Standard mathematical programming techniques do not deal well with this problem, as they may get stuck in local optima. The use of such statistical optimization techniques as genetic algorithms and simulated annealing is a fundamental development. Genetic algorithms are an adaptive method that evolve a population of encoded solutions according to rules inspired by genetic evolution. Invented in the 1960s by John Holland at the University of Michigan, genetic algorithms are now finding applications in optimization problems.

Another development is the use of hybridization techniques to dynamically allocate the best methodology to the solution of an optimization problem. A hybrid method might, for example, start with a genetic algorithm procedure to explore the global landscape and switch to a mathematical programming method for fine-tuning. Hybridization is at the forefront of adaptive methodologies.

Lastly, the development of problem description languages is facilitating the statement of a business modeling problem, making the process easy and intuitive. In the past, optimization problems required specialized staff to understand the problem and code it in a suitable form. Using problem-solving methods, it has become possible to simplify the process.

The above advances have found their way to the market in off-the-shelf products. The software package Evolver from the Seattle-based Axcelis combines genetic algorithms and the Excel spreadsheet, allowing users to take advantage of the former without the need to program them.

The business modeling package Quantum Leap from Quantum Development combines a problem description language with optimization engines based on the hybridization of different optimization algorithms, including genetic algorithms and simulated annealing. The power of Quantum Leap is two-pronged: the optimization engine achieves high performance by choosing the methodology best suited to each problem; the business description language simplifies the task of formalizing the business problem.

Products such as Quantum Leap are the new frontier of problem solving in financial applications. Taking advantage of the large amount of computing power now available, they combine a user-friendly problem-solving interface with powerful optimization methodologies. At a major insurance company, optimization problems that took days to solve are now solved in minutes using Quantum Leap. This is a qualitative change in the way companies can handle a vast array of financial problems. IBM calls this type of product "middleware," because it serves as a building block, facilitating applications development. Ben C. Barnes, vice president for marketing, development, and strategy at IBM's RISC System/6000 Division, believes middleware will play a fundamental role in the development of financial analytics in the near future, impacting the financial sector as a whole.

A new important development in optimization follows the lines of genetic programming. Genetic programming is a technique invented by Stanford University's John Koza to evolve programs according to a genetic paradigm. The basic idea of genetic programming is to rate the "fitness" of programs through a numerical function defined over a number of structural characteristics of programs; each value of the fitness function corresponds to a specific program. Genetic algorithms can then be used to optimize this function and find the "best" program. In other words, genetic programming uses genetic optimization techniques to find optimal programs.

The idea of genetic programming has been applied to evolve neural networks and other types of algorithms. For instance, genetic programming will optimize a function defined over the topology of a neural network in function of some objective. By applying genetic optimization to the rating function, neural networks change structure and evolve towards better ones.

The concepts of genetic programming can be applied to evolve financial applications. First Quadrant uses genetic algorithms to improve their portfolio of models for stock selection, currency, and tactical asset allocation. David Leinweber, a managing director and head of research at the Pasadena, California-based company, explains that genetic algorithms were used to make the choice of variables in their models and how these variables are transformed. In applications such as these, genetic algorithms help determine the optimal type and number of factors to be used. Dr. Leinweber estimates that, since the start up of their use in 1992, genetic algorithms have improved the average performance of their models by 50 basis points per annum, a significant result. A quantitative asset manager with over $18bn in institutional assets under management, First Quadrant earmarks approximately one-third of its revenue for research in advanced methodologies.

The type of work being done at First Quadrant is an example of a momentous change that is bringing quantitative evaluations to every sector of financial analysis. New optimization techniques, namely genetic algorithms, and problem description methods allow handling quantitatively problems that, only a few years ago, were thought to be completely outside the possibility of automatic quantitative analysis.

3.5 High-performance computing

Computational finance is a numerically intensive computational process. Differential equations describing diffusion processes need to be solved with suitable numerical methods, such as Monte Carlo techniques. Alternative techniques such as binomial lattices imply the evaluation of a large number of possible scenarios, i.e., the evolution paths of interest rates. These processes are numerically intensive. Running optimization cycles over a portfolio of securities is also numerically intensive. Most of these tasks also need to be executed quickly. Using traditional mainframes, financial analytics might take hours to execute. More powerful computer hardware cuts execution times significantly. An objective of many financial firms interviewed is to make pricing evaluations a real-time tool for traders.

The computation-intensive nature of financial analytics was underlined in studies by Stavros Zenios of the Wharton School of Economics. A pioneer in the use of parallel machines for computing prices of complex securities, Prof. Zenios worked at Wharton's Hermes Laboratory, developing financial models of the type now used by Prudential Securities.

According to Erik Carlson, director of strategic analytics and research at Prudential Securities, one of the major issues at the firm is the speed required to make evaluations. Prudential's objective was to be able to evaluate a security over the space of a telephone call and to run optimizations for risk management overnight. These considerations raise the issue of the computing power required by financial analytics.

Prudential Securities was among the first in the financial community to use parallel supercomputing power. Since 1990, the company has installed a 100-node Intel Paragon, a 232-node Intel Hypercube, and more recently an IBM RISC System/6000 SP, in addition to a cluster of RS/6000 workstations. Designed with internal redundancies, these systems are linked to the backbone trading system based on DEC mainframes. The whole system is transparent to users. Prudential has been able to cut computing time for pricing tasks from several hours on mainframes to about 20 seconds on parallel machines, achieving the objective of real-time evaluation.

Prudential Securities has a large amount of computing power by any standard. Dr. Carlson considers this type of power necessary if real-time evaluation of securities and fast turnaround of optimization problems are the objective. Other financial firms have also purchased supercomputers. Merrill Lynch, Freddie Mac, and Atlantic Portfolio and Analytics Management have, for example, installed Cray vector supercomputers.

The use of supercomputers is also impacting risk management. This is the view of Alp Kerestecioglu, partner and director of research at Atlantic Portfolio Analytics & Management (APAM). Dr. Kerestecioglu believes that, by allowing large simulation programs that evaluate risk by developing alternative scenarios as opposed to only parameters, supercomputers have changed the way risk management is performed. The Orlando, Florida-based firm uses a Cray supercomputer to run one of the largest portfolio optimization programs in the industry.

Not all firms have chosen to install supercomputers. Morgan Stanley, for instance, has some 8,500 workstations that collectively supply a massive amount of computing power. Other major financial firms also have a preference for individual workstations. First Quadrant uses parallel networks of workstations, a configuration they judge gives a particularly good price/performance ratio.

Regardless of the hardware platform chosen — vector supercomputers, parallel computers, parallel networks — the financial sector has become a major user of high-performance computing. The need to make evaluations in real time and to run large-scale optimization applications are behind the push to increase computing power.

3.6 Financial engineering tools

Financial computer-aided design (CAD) is a recent development born from the need to engineer complex derivative products. A number of off-the-shelf software packages are now available as financial CAD packages. They are used to structure and price complex transactions, running financial simulations and engineering the contractual part of the deal.

Financial engineering is an engineering task in its own right. It starts with a functional description of a product and ends with the product's structural description. This objective is achieved through a search implemented by coupling intuition with problem-solving methods. Kevin Holley, head of artificial intelligence (AI) at Morgan Stanley, remarks that making this process faster and more efficient is a major goal at Morgan Stanley. The firm uses AI techniques to guide financial engineers in their search for products that respond to specific functional characteristics.

Rod Beckstroem, founder of C*ATS, a Palo Alto-based company supplying capital markets software, sees financial CAD as a major development that will shape the financial industry of the future. The key to the development of financial CAD is, he believes, dynamic object-oriented techniques. He sees the complex legal contracts that make up a derivative as a network of objects in an object-oriented methodology. This concept allows for the rapid development of new derivative products, building the right network of objects. New products can be developed internally by the bank or by a third party with the CAD tools. New instruments can then be processed through a consistent set of risk management, credit, accounting, and other products.

The concept of object-oriented methodology is attractive for financial firms that have seen software development costs skyrocket over the last few years. One Wall Street firm alone added 800 persons to their development staff last year. Historically, most of the large firms have developed their own software, making it difficult to introduce commercial packages. However, with the growing need to control costs, object-oriented techniques are an important development. They allow internally developed programs and commercial packages to coexist as objects linked in a network.

3.7 Intelligent man-machine interfaces

A trader is always in the situation of having to look at many complex screens at the same time, trying to make sense of all of them at once. With the speed of calculation of today's computers, presenting results has become a serious problem. Most major firms interviewed indicated that they had ongoing research programs on how to improve the human interface with financial analytics.

Morgan Stanley's head of artificial intelligence, Kevin Holley, says that exploring efficient ways to present results is a very important line of research at the firm. True three-dimensional presentation techniques are being considered as a way to enable their traders to evaluate a situation at a glance. Other large Wall Street firms share the same preoccupation and are exploring similar techniques.

Commercial software developers such as Toronto-based Algorithmics are sensitive to the problem of visualizing results. The company's president, Ron Dembo, views graphics as a unified language that gives common understanding to concepts such as risk. Algorithmics has chosen color bars and graphs with an animation facility for graphics presentation. Visuals can be used not only to represent output data, but also to modify input.

Machine-learning techniques can play an important role in building user-friendly presentations, creating human interfaces that automatically adapt to the user. A major line of research in this area was originated at Carnegie Mellon University. Researchers there introduced the notion of the SILKy interface able to handle Speech, Images, Language, and Knowledge. The objective is to produce human interfaces that adapt to the user and are able to integrate missing or wrong information, as well as interacting in a more efficient way through a combination of language and image.

A team led by Tom Mitchell, professor at the university's School of Computer Science, introduced case-based learning techniques to engineer systems that automatically adapt to the preferences and reasoning of their users. A prototype system that works as a meeting scheduler was developed as a proof of concept. These techniques can be helpful in understanding how to best present results on a screen.

Another area of research in man-machine interaction is the use of descriptive programming to implement applications. Financial applications are generally written in procedural languages that specify every step in a procedure. Using AI techniques, descriptive programming allows the user to build his or her own application by simply describing it. David Leinweber, now a managing director at the investment management firm First Quadrant, pioneered these ideas, applying descriptive programming to the development of financial applications.

3.8 Automatic news analysis

Another line of research that emerged from our interviews is the automatic analysis of news. Economists preparing scenarios receive an enormous amount of information, whether in print or over the wires. This information can easily exceed what a specialist can read in a working day, but overlooking some important piece of information might negatively impact the quality of the analysis. Most large firms interviewed such as Morgan Stanley and specialized software houses like The Prediction Company, are presently researching systems for automatic news analysis.

The first goal is to extract what is important from spurious information, i.e., to build an information filter. In the long run, however, more ambitious goals, such as checking the consistency of news, grouping news items according to meaning, detecting statistical trends in the news, or evaluating the impact of news on the market, will be set. The research aim is to develop software systems able to filter incoming news and to offer a scenario of future events based on the most important news items.

In a joint research project, Intelligent Financial Systems (IFS) in Potsdam, Germany, and the Berlin-based J&J Financial Consultants are developing a filtering system that performs fact extraction from financial news using artificial intelligence techniques. Called FINAS — Financial News Analysis System — the system analyzes texts from the news wires, extracting facts in a chosen domain and converting them into a formal representation. IFS is now working on a project to combine news analysis and the extraction of fundamental information with time series analysis.

The complex problem of relating public news to market movements was cited by Charles Goodhart, the Norman Sosnow professor of banking and finance at the London School of Economics. According to Prof. Goodhart, public news is not influencing markets such as the foreign exchange or government bond markets as strongly as one might expect. He remarks that what is important is not news in itself, but the difference between the news and the expectation of the market. As the flow of news is continuous, it is difficult but important to ascertain the effect of each news item. Prof. Goodhart suggests that a better understanding of the interaction between rational agents is needed.

At Erasmus University-Rotterdam, Dirk-Emma Baestaens is conducting research on news analysis. Prof. Baestaens remarks that a major problem is to separate messages confirming the expectation of market participants from the unexpected "true" news. His approach is to explore what combinations of words in the news pages are followed by price behavior that diverges from the expected. The central issue is the determination of the expected market behavior at the time a news flash appears. Prof. Baestaens defines the expected behavior of the market as that revealed by statistical analysis. His research has shown that there are significant correlations between unexpected news and market movements, such as the DEM/USD swap rate. Prof. Baestaens uses a number of linear and non-linear techniques, including neural networks.

3.9 Simulation

Current risk management techniques include analytics and simulation. Analytical techniques are based on a theoretical evaluation of the behavior of financial quantities. As remarked in the previous chapter, analytical techniques are often used to estimate the sensitivity of the derivatives to changes in underlying parameters, usually referred to with Greek letters as *deltas*, *vegas*, *rhos*, and so on, in function of the parameter considered.

An advance in risk management techniques is the use of simulation. Simulation does not attempt to derive analytical relationships between variables, but runs scenarios under many different assumptions, including some extreme potential behavior. The technology of simulation has developed over the last few years due to the availability of low-cost high-performance computers. Blake LeBaron, associate professor of economics at the University of Wisconsin-Madison, believes that simulation, coupled with forecasting models, will play a fundamental role in risk management. He remarks that understanding risk involves simulating scenarios and considers that analytics will not be very helpful in this task.

Alp Kerestecioglu, partner and research director at fixed-income money manager Atlantic Portfolio Analytics & Management (APAM), believes that running simulations is the only sensible way to handle asset management for a firm that holds positions. The Orlando, Florida company runs its optimization programs on a Cray supercomputer. Simulation is central to APAM's business. Dr. Kerestecioglu remarks that they do not handle any product they cannot simulate. The process starts by generating all possible unknowns — interest rates, swap spreads, volatility, security evaluation spreads, etc. — to ascertain the magnitude of uncertainty. The universe is then evaluated, running simulations to understand what could go wrong and to identify investment opportunities. The whole process is optimized.

First Quadrant's David Leinweber agrees that simulation will play an ever greater role in risk management. Dr. Leinweber believes, however, that simulation requires caution, as there are many potential traps and sources of bias that can distort simulated performance.

There are commercially available products for performing simulation for managing risk. Toronto-based Algorithmics supplies one such product. The company's vice president for financial engineering, Michael Zerbs, shares the opinion that the complexity of simulation programs must be reduced. He looks to intelligent techniques to reduce this complexity by restricting simulations to the most promising areas of analysis.

Another approach is being explored at the Banca Commerciale Italiana, where Umberto Cherubini is using Kohonen maps to cluster simulation paths according to similarity rules. By taking only representatives from each cluster, clustering could lead to a substantial reduction in the number of simulation paths required.

It is fair to conclude that, in the opinion of many researchers and practitioners, simulation will be the key technology in risk management. Simulation alone, however, will not suffice. Intelligent techniques will be combined with simulation in order to reduce the combinatorial explosion of the number of simulation paths to be considered.

References
Baestaens, D.-E. and W. van den Bergh, "The Marginal Contribution of News to the DEM/USD Swap Rate," *Neural Network World*, Vol. 5, No. 4, 1995, Editor M. Novak, IDG, Prague.

Barucci, E., U. Cherubini and L. Landi, "No-Arbitrage Asset Pricing with Neural Networks under Stochastic Volatility," University of Florence, 1995.

Black, F., "Noise," *Journal of Finance*, 41: 529-543.

Leinweber, D.J. and R.D. Arnott, "Quantitative and Computational Innovation in Investment Management," *Journal of Portfolio Management*, Vol. 21, No. 2, Winter 1995.

Lo, A.W. and T. Poggio, "A Nonparametric Approach to Pricing and Hedging Derivative Securities Via Learning Networks," *Working Paper No. RPCF-1005-94*, MIT Sloan School of Management.

Lo, A.W. and J. Wang, "Implementing Option Pricing Models When Asset Returns Are Predictable," *Working Paper No. RPCF-1001-93R1*, MIT Sloan School of Management.

Makivic, M., "Path Integral Monte Carlo Method for Valuation of Derivative Securities: Algorithms and Parallel Implementations," *Neural Network World*, Vol. 5, No. 4, 1995, Editor M. Novak, IDG, Prague.

Zenios, S.A., editor, *Financial Optimization*, Cambridge University Press, Cambridge, 1993.

4. MODELS OF NON-EQUILIBRIUM MARKETS AND NON-LINEAR METHODS

4.1 A new generation of models

Financial research and practice are now entering a new stage characterized by a greater use of empirical data in both theory and model building. This change bears consequences for the theory as well as the practice of finance. Chapter 1 outlined recent theoretical developments, including the recognition that financial markets are made up of heterogeneous agents with different risk profiles, motivations, and expectations. Neither equally nor fully informed, these agents interact in complex ways. However, as remarked by University of Wisconsin professor of economics Blake LeBaron, the empirical side of research on economy and finance is ahead of the theoretical side. While research results offer partial explanations, there is yet no tenable comprehensive theory to explain non-equilibrium market dynamics.

As a consequence, there is no new generation of financial models backed by firm theory. Financial models originating in the new framework are based on adaptive computational methods. New technological developments bypass the process of theory formation by using generalized mathematical models that are fit to data through a process of optimization.

There is a vast research agenda on adaptive models. Adaptive computational methods are being applied principally to 1) understand the structure of the market, and 2) make profitable forecasts for trading. An impulse to research was given by Zurich-based

Olsen & Associates in a recent move to make available to the academic community the company's 20 million filtered FX bid-ask quotes collected since 1986.

Work being done at the Santa Fe Institute to develop an abstract model of the market made up of learning agents was cited above, as was work being done at Carnegie Mellon University to integrate econometric models with adaptive methods. A good deal of research work is presently devoted to finding non-equilibrium explanations for stylized facts discovered through the statistical analysis of market data. This research includes attempts to develop structural theories as well as efforts to apply adaptive methods. The explanation of the clustering of volatilities by the ARCH and GARCH methods developed by Engle and Bollerslev respectively are notable successes of this type of research. New versions of these models are currently being added.

The effort to understand the market through adaptive methods is not limited to academia. Guillaume van der Linden, head of trading risk management at ING Bank remarks that though the Amsterdam bank adheres to the random walk theory of financial markets, they are using neural networks to find patterns of and explanations for market behavior. Robin Griffiths, chief technical analyst at James Capel in London, developed a neural network-based system for forecasting the Footsie index. Mr. Griffiths finds that neural networks are good at identifying the key variables that influence the market. They are concentrating their efforts in neural network technology on understanding what factors are the most important for describing the market.

4.2 Technological continuity

Although the new framework is conceptually different from the classical one, there is technological continuity in the path of adaptive non-linear methods from the classical to the new dynamic framework. This should come as no surprise: in most scientific revolutions, previous laws and concepts remain approximations.

Paul Refenes, senior research fellow at the London Business School's department of decision science, remarks that conventional financial analytics makes simplifying assumptions that lead to linear relationships, such as the APT (Arbitrage Pricing Theory) or CAPM asset pricing models. With the new adaptive methods, these simplifying assumptions might be dropped, replaced by more realistic non-linear functions. Additional forecastability can be extracted from the market, replacing white noise with more meaningful statistical estimates.

Suran Goonatilake, a researcher at University College London's computer science department, is an advocate of combining adaptive methodologies and existing financial analytics procedures. He observes that most successful systems to date are those that have used existing financial analytics as input.

The Prediction Company's Norman Packard believes that the broad notion of diffusion processes key to today's financial analytics will remain. Forecasting methods will be superimposed on this conceptual framework, creating a new generation of computational finance that will exploit the possibilities offered by forecasting.

4.3 Non-linear adaptive methods in computational finance

The adaptive computational approach builds models by fitting generalized models to sample data. An important feature of these models is the non-linearity of the relationships they describe. Non-linearity entails a higher level of complexity in models, but offers superior explanatory power.

The key issue of the adaptive approach is generalization, i.e., the reconstruction of an entire function from a number of examples. Adaptive methods use general mathematical models for reconstructing functions. Models include a number of free parameters determined through a learning process that fits models to data through an optimization procedure. From a strictly mathematical point of view, there is no solution to the generalization problem. Given any number of examples of a function, there is no way to predict with certainty the remaining values. The ability to generalize is based on some physical assumptions that constrain the spectrum of possible values and functions.

The success of adaptive methods is based on matching the complexity of the problem, the flexibility of the models' algorithms, and the amount and quality of available data. A theoretical understanding of the problem under consideration might prove to be essential for the choice of the algorithm's structure.

Generalization is a key step in forecasting. The objective is to model time series by constructing a function that generates future data as a function of past data. If long series of data are available, there are many samples of the relationship between sets of data and their successors. From these samples, and with suitable generalization procedures, it is possible to reconstruct the functional dependency of data from their predecessors and use these functions to predict future outcomes.

A wide variety of methods are used. Some, such as neural networks, are universal function approximators, i.e., they can in principle be used to approximate any function. The statement that neural networks are universal function approximators is much weaker than it might at first seem. It states that for any function there is a neural network able to approximate it with arbitrary precision. It does not, however, indicate how to construct such a network. There is, nevertheless, no *a priori* limitation in the use of neural networks.

Other methods depend on specific theoretical assumptions. The ARCH and GARCH family of statistical methods, for example, are used to model phenomena that show a specific clustering of volatility. These are adaptive methods insofar as they are fitted to data, but the functional dependency they implement has specific theoretical motivations. They reach superior performance in the narrow fields where they are applicable.

Although a fundamental innovation, adaptive computational methods lack a solid foundation. Many persons interviewed for this book voiced interest in the adaptive approach, but expressed some concern. Maureen O'Hara, professor of management and finance at Cornell University, remarks that adaptive methods are very useful at finding patterns, but cannot grow beyond pattern recognition. GARCH methods, she says, look at patterns for price but ignore volume. She argues for a deeper theoretical understanding.

Adaptive methods can, however, succeed where humans fail. The University of Wisconsin's Blake LeBaron notes that adaptive methods can show a significant advantage over the human observer in areas such as finding patterns in multivariate series.

In the present scenario of computational finance, adaptive methods provide relatively simple mathematical models of data, most often time series, even in the absence of theoretical knowledge. Their justification lies essentially in out-of-sample validation, i.e., from the demonstration that they effectively work in a large number of cases outside of the training examples.

4.4 Forecasting in a non-equilibrium framework

From a practitioner's point of view, the hallmark of adaptive methods is their ability to forecast time series. A good share of the excitement in the financial community for methods such as neural networks comes from the possibility that they might help generate excess returns. It is therefore appropriate to review the position of forecasting in the new framework.

In the classical view, efficient markets react immediately to news, incorporating new information in security prices. A market is efficient because it implements without delay optimal decision rules according to some asset valuation scheme and using all available information. This is expressed through the notion that unanticipated returns are martingales under the qualification that returns can be anticipated by an asset pricing scheme.

The practical consequence is that the forecasting of financial quantities, volatilities and prices alike, can be done within the classical framework, but that there are upper bounds to trading or optimization strategies. These upper bounds can be approximately stated by saying that high returns are tied to high risk. This is true only under a number of assumptions; the statement of efficiency can become very complex in the general case. The notion that it is impossible to beat the market needs refinement if one wants to define precisely the sense in which the market can or cannot be beaten.

Suppose that an algorithm makes a forecast that shows a particularly good return for some security. The classical theory maintains that this high level of return must be correlated with a high level of risk according to theoretically known relationships. If not, the market would spot the opportunity and the price advantage would disappear. The market itself implements the optimal forecast and optimal decision rules. The dynamics of price adjustments are not modeled in the classical equilibrium framework.

The substantial difference in the handling of forecasting in the new framework is the consideration of the non-equilibrium dynamics of the market. The new framework recognizes that, due to the intrinsic structure of the market, there are price movements that do not correspond to a rational evaluation of risk. Market pricing is not optimal, as in the classical sense, but is subject to large and partially predictable fluctuations under forces that include the fundamental heterogeneity of market participants.

Because the new framework establishes no firm risk/return

relationship, the forecasting of high returns does not necessarily entail the market consensus of large corresponding deviations. As fluctuations in the price of securities are much larger than expected returns over short periods, forecasting holds the promise of excess returns. In fact, in a trading day stock prices might experience fluctuations in the range of 1%, while the corresponding long-term return is in the range of 0.05%.

It should be noted that there cannot be any true arbitrage opportunity in the market. Arbitrage means that arbitrary gains can be made through leverage. However, because any forecast entails uncertainty as regards the forecast itself, no true arbitrage exists. There are other considerations as well. Investing large funds in a trading strategy would have large-scale effects on prices. These effects would in turn run the risk of offsetting potential gains.

The above considerations underline the fact that defining excess return is not a straightforward matter. In a non-equilibrium setting, there is no arbitrage, as there are realistic constraints to any possible gain. On the other hand, agents realize gains that do not correspond to the maximization of their respective utility functions but imply differences in their forecasting abilities. This is, however, a rather difficult concept to quantify precisely.

There is yet no global theoretical framework to explain non-equilibrium movements. The eventual limits of forecastability and the consequent maximum possible gains are, therefore, not known. What is known is that a number of methods allow one to earn returns in excess of the returns that would be made with classical models. This has been demonstrated in a variety of trading situations, in the FX market as well as the stock market. It has been shown empirically that there are profitable, albeit complex, trading rules. It is important to understand that it is always a matter of a *contest* between different models.

The risk — theoretical or empirical — involved in forecasting is not known. This is a critical problem for dynamic forecasting methods. No theoretical framework allows a sure prediction of risk; forecasting procedures can be judged only on the basis of historical performance.

A number of methods for evaluating the quality of forecasts have been developed. These methods take into account time averages of returns and volatilities. They examine how a forecasting procedure has fared by comparing the returns it generated with the returns of a portfolio of similar risk in the classical sense. But this is really like comparing apples and oranges: one is a measure of risk given by estimates that are valid only within the classical framework; the other is a measure of risk as a statistical estimate valid only if the statistical assumptions are correct. Ultimately, we might have meaningless results.

These remarks point to the fact that the use of non-linear adaptive methods in finance should be clearly understood within a given theoretical framework. If non-linear adaptive methods are used as forecasting devices, it is clear that problems might arise in evaluating their performance.

Most academics interviewed remarked that earning excess returns by forecasting is not easy: the market is quite efficient, non-linear relationships are difficult to ascertain, and patterns once discovered tend to go away. John Moody, associate professor at the Oregon Graduate Institute's department of computer science and vice president of the Neural Information Processing Systems Foundation, remarks that it is already possible to see the consequences of forecasting methodologies in a number of less liquid markets where profitability has been reduced.

Cornell University's Maureen O'Hara remarks that once a pattern is found it rapidly disappears as investors exploit it. It was, however, also remarked that as opportunities disappear, new ones could be found. The quest for better techniques is a moving target.

Blake LeBaron, associate professor of economics at the University of Wisconsin, believes that there are two possible future scenarios: either forecasting techniques based on adaptive methods will make markets more efficient, wiping out the last bit of forecastability, or, alternatively, there will be no convergence on technology as old models die out and new ones are continuously proposed.

Most academics recognize the attraction of forecasting for large trading organizations. Among practitioners, there are strong advocates. Richard Olsen, Oxford-trained economist and founder of Olsen & Associates, believes that the heterogeneous structure of the market creates forecastability by responding to news in forecastable ways. Markets do not react immediately to news, but show forecastable delayed responses. These, Dr. Olsen maintains, carry over time.

References

Arthur, W.B., "On the Evolution of Complexity," *The Santa Fe Institute Paper*, No. 93-11-070, 1993.

Arthur, W.B., "On Learning and Adaptation in the Economy," Working Paper No. 92-07-38, *Santa Fe Institute Economics Research Program*.

Breeden, J.L. and N.H. Packard, "A Learning Algorithm for Optimal Representations of Experimental Data," *Technical Report CCSR-92-11*, University of Illinois Urbana-Champaign.

Brock, H.W., J. Lakonishok and B. LeBaron, "Simple Technical Trading Rules and the Stochastic Properties of Stock Returns," *Journal of Finance*, 47, No. 5: 1731-1764, 1992.

Packard, N.H., "A Genetic Learning Algorithm for the Analysis of Complex Data," *Complex Systems*, Vol. 4: 543-572, 1990.

Refenes, A.N., editor, *Neural Networks in the Capital Markets*, Proceedings from the International Workshop on Neural Networks in the Capital Markets, London Business School, 1995.

Weigend, A.S. and N.A. Gershenfeld, editors, *Time Series Prediction: Forecasting the Future and Understanding the Past*, Addison-Wesley, Reading, MA, 1994.

PART II
IMPLEMENTATION

5. INVESTMENT MANAGEMENT

5.1 Styles of investment management

Investment management is the process through which money is managed. Ultimately, the rationale behind investment is the ability of the economy to create wealth. On a large scale, investments are made because the economy is able to pay a return as a consequence of activities that increase global wealth.

In the classical view of finance, securities are fairly priced as efficient markets set a security's price as a trade-off between the expected rate of return and the risk related to the return. Investors select the risk/return profile of their choice.

Investment is, however, also associated with a more speculative view of finance where funds are managed in function of information not in the public domain or sheer manipulation. Fortunes have been made — and lost — on speculation. Speculators act on the belief that they have a knowledge advantage over the market or that they can induce market movements.

The rapid diffusion of communication and the globalization of trades have made markets more efficient and speculation more difficult. Modern portfolio theory is based on the notion that markets are basically efficient in their processing of information and that mispricings allow only modest gains over the global performance of the market. At the same time, the investment industry has increased many times over. It was estimated that at the end of 1993 the worldwide investable market portfolio totalled $33.7 trillion. Even marginal gains can be translated into huge profits.

In the practice of finance, the majority of funds are managed with professional criteria under a variety of styles that match investors' preferences towards risk. The basic styles of investment management can be characterized as passive or active to various degrees. The passive investment management style signals a close adherence to the efficient market hypothesis (EMH). The fundamental underlying belief is that there is a close relationship between risk and returns, a relationship fairly determined by the market and not to be improved upon. The active style signals the belief that 1) the market undergoes frequent and sizable changes, and that 2) the market might show inefficiencies from which active trading strategies might profit.

Managers of the passive style use, if any, models that adhere to the classical notions of efficient asset pricing. They select portfolios that come as close as possible to the market portfolio by taking appropriate market indexes. Managers of the active style might use a variety of different models and techniques. Technologies used might still be within the EMH framework or they might genuinely exploit true dynamic effects.

With the relaxation of some of the tenets of the efficient market hypothesis and the development of scientific investment management techniques, new styles of fund and investment management are emerging. Based on a pure technological information-gathering process, the new styles attempt to exploit market fluctuations on a large scale. They not only exploit deviations in the normal process of returns generation, but rely on market fluctuations independent of the process of wealth creation. The currency funds are a good example.

New types of investment, particularly in the most liquid and/or volatile markets, are being created. These are based on the ability of technology to forecast price movements. There are a number of examples of this type of investment management, including the OIS Benchmark Fund based on Olsen & Associates' trading model technology, and funds engineered by The Prediction Company for Swiss Bank Corporation.

5.2 Investment performance

Literature, academic and non-academic alike, reports no convincing evidence of investment managers' ability to earn excess returns. The notion of efficient markets was, in fact, motivated by the failure of money managers to produce excess returns. Two considerations should be made. First, many large funds engage in operations that affect the market. These funds gain a controlling stake in companies and might engineer strategies to manage their investment "at the source." Big investment firms can and do play an important role in the strategic management of companies. Second, bearing higher risk produces fluctuations in one's own wealth but, in the long run, higher cumulative profits. Studies have demonstrated that stocks with a higher risk yield higher returns. In evaluating performance, the effective long-term risk should be taken into consideration.

Investment styles based on forecasting raise a number of questions. One question is, obviously, why an approach based on anticipating price movements should give better results than an approach based on understanding the wealth-generation process. Why, for instance, should it be possible to earn higher returns betting on the future course of exchange rates than investing in the shares of a wealth-generating company? There is presently no theoretical answer. That markets show large fluctuations is an empirically known fact. In any relatively small time interval, fluctuations are much larger than expected economic growth. In the stock market, for example, price changes in the range of 1% during a trading day are not uncommon; the corresponding expected return might, as mentioned, be in the range of 0.05%.

It is the possibility of exploiting a sizable fraction of this volatility that has spurred most attempts to devise investment strategies based on short-term forecastability. The consequences for finance and the economy are difficult to call. A thorough understanding in mathematical terms of the consequences on the market of new decision-making approaches is beyond present theoretical possibilities. The classical theory, and most extensions of it, represent investors as utility maximizers. Introducing a more complex and articulate decision-making process is a difficult endeavor that research is only now beginning to tackle.

Proponents of the forecast-based investment style are not uniform in their evaluation of how forecasting will affect the market and the relative benefits. Some believe that a forecasting approach is due to the intrinsic heterogeneity of the market and that forecasting methods will not wipe out the benefits of forecasting. A notable proponent of this view is the Zurich-based Olsen & Associates. Others, such as the Santa Fe, New Mexico-based Prediction Company, believe that secrecy is essential, as forecasting exploits differentials in information and knowledge that would be destroyed by the diffusion of the technology.

Most of the new investment management techniques are undertaken in secrecy; there is little reliable data on performance. This makes it difficult to judge if the technologies are delivering what they promised.

5.3 Depth of use of technology
Investment management is still performed largely through personal contacts and human judgment. As remarked by Davis Jessop, a Cambridge-trained mathematician and quantitative fund manager at Morgan Grenfell Asset Management, the selection of stocks at the London firm is done through visits to investment targets. Some 2,000 visits are made yearly to companies the firm

is considering as potential investments. Morgan Grenfell manages some $50bn in assets.

A number of technologies are complementing human judgment in portfolio management, serving either as a management tool to evaluate risk, a decision-support tool, or as a fully automated investment management procedure. Among the techniques used are multifactor models, time series analysis, and simulation.

At Morgan Grenfell, multifactor models are used to allow managers to perform risk analysis on their portfolios. At Schroder Investment Management, a London-based low-risk fund management firm with $90bn in assets under management, the use of multifactor models to analyze risk on portfolios has become increasingly common over the last two to three years. Pension funds, says investment manager Andrew Simpson, are increasingly requiring the quantification of risk.

Atlantic Portfolio Analytics & Management (APAM) goes one step further. According to partner and research director Alp Kerestecioglu, the Orlando, Florida-based fixed-income money manager limits their investments to those that can be analyzed mathematically with simulation algorithms. Using a Cray supercomputer, APAM runs large simulation and optimization programs.

Quantitative mathematical methods are also being used to direct timely shifts in major segments of portfolios: among asset classes, between equity styles, in currency hedging, in yield curve strategies, in primary bond markets. First Quadrant is a case in point. The Pasadena, California firm uses proprietary multifactor models refined through the application of genetic programming techniques.

5.4 Investment technology
Within the classical framework, investment technologies

include primarily multifactor models and, more recently, simulation. Multifactor models forecast risk and returns for each security and optimize portfolios with appropriate techniques. Portfolios are periodically checked and rebalanced. These methods adhere to a risk/return optimization policy, but maintain that there is considerable potential for identifying portfolios with a favorable risk/return profile. As already seen, there are ample opportunities for using adaptive methods within this framework. First Quadrant is an example of an asset management firm that uses advanced adaptive optimization, namely genetic algorithms, for designing optimal multifactor models. Software company BARRA uses non-linear GARCH techniques for forecasting volatilities. Neural networks have also found application here.

One company that has been successful in applying neural network and non-linear statistics technologies is Fidelity Investments, the world's largest fund management company with $258bn of assets under management. With a successful track record in applying traditional analysis and techniques — Fidelity has been producing returns consistently above the S&P average — the firm is a pioneer in the use of machine-learning methods for portfolio management. Bradford Lewis, a portfolio manager at Fidelity, started applying neural networks to select stocks in 1992. The neural network application developed by Mr. Lewis has been highly publicized because of its consistently good performance. Inside Fidelity itself, Mr. Lewis's experience is considered an important proof of the concept for machine learning in portfolio management.

Significantly, an objective of Fidelity's research team is to identify applications in fund management where machine-learning techniques might be applied. Stephen Campbell, vice president in charge of the technical research unit, says the firm's attitude is very pragmatic. If new techniques demonstrate superior results, they are taken "live" to prove themselves. If results are good, the pilot is extended to wider portions of the business. Fidelity's evaluation is that it is now possible to gain a slight improvement in returns on stock portfolios using forecasting implemented with machine-learning techniques. Even slight improvements, however, translate into sizable gains.

It is interesting to note that these gains are being achieved despite the constraint of being fully invested in the equity capital markets. A leading investment management firm, Fidelity is not generally free to convert large portions of its funds into cash and to use timing signals to trade. Mr. Campbell thinks that using neural networks to issue timing signals to trade might produce much higher returns. However, he considers this a strategy open only to small firms or individuals who are able to step out of the market and maintain large cash positions when required.

While the overall impact of machine-learning technologies is still limited, Mr. Campbell believes that these technologies will show significant performance improvement in the future. According to Fidelity's technical and quantitative research head, one of the most important issues is the availability of data: as algorithms will be to a large extent equivalent, the major factors determining success will be the quantity and quality of data, and the ability of the portfolio manager to preprocess the data.

A different approach is being taken by Atlantic Portfolio Analytics & Management (APAM), a $7bn fixed-income money manager. The firm has eschewed artificial intelligence techniques and financial analytics, using supercomputer-based simulations in managing portfolios. The reason, says Alp Kerestecioglu, partner and research director, is the need to get all uncertainties upfront. The company generates millions of scenarios to reduce risk and optimize portfolios.

We are now witnessing the emergence of applications of non-linear adaptive methods in investment management that call for deviations from the efficient market hypothesis. Typically, these methods require an understanding of the time dynamic of security prices. Investment strategies are based on the belief that there is no upper bound to the forecasting of risk/return as imposed by market efficiency: high returns are not necessarily correlated with a high level of risk.

The Prediction Company in Santa Fe, New Mexico represents a ground-breaking experiment in computer-based forecasting for futures trading. The company was founded by two of the scientists that opened the field of chaos theory, Doyne Farmer and Norman Packard. Their pioneering academic work on chaos led them to the conclusion that it was possible to make a profit predicting the course of products traded as futures contracts.

To test their ideas live, The Prediction Company made an agreement with the Chicago-based securities firm O'Connor & Associates under which the latter would provide funds to be traded and profits would be shared. Funds allocated to trading would be increased according to profitability. Although O'Connor was successively bought by Swiss Bank Corporation, the cooperation continues.

The Prediction Company uses very sophisticated forecasting technologies that stem from its founders' work on chaos theory. Using past values of time series — those to be forecasted plus other correlated series — The Prediction Company performs a state-space embedding where sets of values of the series are used as coordinates of points in a state space. This operation is useful in detecting the geometrical structure of the trajectory of the point in the state space. The key idea is that different regions in the embedded state space have different levels of forecastability, different dimensionalities, and, therefore, require different models. Their modeling is a collection of models that work in different regions of the series. The embedding starts with a very high dimensionality, perhaps hundreds of dimensions, that are then reduced for each local region.

The notions and the actual mechanics of The Prediction Company's modeling are very complex. Managing a large dimensionality of the embedding, detecting areas of local forecastability, and switching from one model to another are complex tasks. A team of 15 scientists and software developers choose the modeling techniques — including neural networks, statistical methods, and genetic algorithms — most appropriate for each problem. The objective is to make the model-building process completely automatic using genetic algorithms. Presently, however, models are created with human intervention.

The highly sophisticated forecasting techniques designed by The Prediction Company have been successful at least to some extent. Their partnership continues, an indication that forecasting results are positive. Accordingly to Dr. Packard, the major problem presently is not the statistical success of forecasting but the variance of predictions. In other words, one can certainly make money over time, but the residual risk that local losses might exceed credit limits is still high.

In Europe the OIS Benchmark Fund, a managed currency fund, was created using Olsen & Associates' trading model technology. Open to the public as an investment, the fund works by trading currencies following the recommendations of the O&A trading models. It is another example of completely automated investment management.

References

Coggin, T.D. and F.J. Fabozzi, *Equity Style Management*, Frank J. Fabozzi Associates, New Hope, PA, 1995.

Frauendorfer, K., "The Stochastic Programming Extension of the

Markowitz Approach," *Neural Network World*, Vol. 5, No. 4, 1995, Editor M. Novak, IDG, Prague.

Zenios, S.A., editor, *Financial Optimization*, Cambridge University Press, Cambridge, 1993.

6. TRADING

Although managing assets involves trading, entities that actually trade are not necessarily those that manage investments. The previous chapter covered advanced technologies in asset management; this chapter covers adaptive technologies in trading.

6.1 Trading as process control

Trading involves a strategy of interaction with the environment as perceived by traders. Forecasting, in and of itself, is not sufficient to ensure profitable trading. It offers conditional probability distributions that are only one component of a trading strategy, the objective of which is to extract profit from marginal forecastability edges.

Directional forecasting of foreign exchange rates, for instance, might prove to be statistically right only slightly above 50% of the time. Real numbers are effectively in this range as markets are not grossly inefficient. The problem of trading is to translate this marginal forecastability into a profit within the agreed upon limits of risk. Because the action of trading itself might influence the market, thereby changing the price scenario, trading strategies require monitoring of the market and an understanding of market movements in a probabilistic environment.

Interviewees remarked that the role of forecasting should be considered within the global problem of designing trading strategies. Northwestern University's Tim Bollerslev thinks that profitable trading on directional forecasts depends more on how one trades on the forecast than on the forecast itself. Christian Dunis, head of the quantitative research and trading group (QRT) at Chemical Bank in London, remarks that the interest is in *trading* models and observes that forecasting should be integrated into a trading strategy. Unless linked to a sound trading model, Mr. Dunis says, it is possible to have a good forecasting model that loses money. Olsen & Associates, a Zurich-based supplier of on-line forecasts for the foreign exchange market, stresses the need to integrate trading recommendations with adequate trading rules.

In his paper "Nerds on Wall Street," David Leinweber, a managing director and head of research at First Quadrant, likens traders to robots: both have to execute strategies based on perceptions and evaluations. Dr. Leinweber believes that there are numerous advantages to an adaptive strategy of control based on a hierarchy of instruction levels, each level related to a certain type of task.

The question of implementing trading rules as process control was posed to academics and practitioners alike. A number of financial institutions we talked to have as a priority the automation of the trading process. Many, however, remain skeptical as to the possibility of ever fully replacing man by machines. The impossibility of designing a trading system to meet all contingencies was widely cited as the motivation for the skepticism. Blake LeBaron, of the University of Wisconsin-Madison, notes that trading rules have typically been implemented by people. However, new technologies are able to handle increasing quantities of data, series of data, simultaneously. The real question, Prof. LeBaron believes, is how process control will be implemented, i.e., in suggestive or hostile fashion.

6.2 Trading on forecasts
Forecasting methodologies have attracted the attention of

proprietary traders in areas like foreign exchange where they offer the prospect of exploiting differentials between the present market price and the forecast price. But forecasting is also beneficial in advising clients and executing orders.

There is agreement that the FX market represents one of the most interesting opportunities for forecasting methods: the market is highly liquid and the volume of trading large, in the range of $1 trillion a day; rates are for the most part driven by market forces; and many of the traders are technical traders.

In Europe, the Zurich-based Olsen & Associates has pioneered forecasting methods in the area of foreign exchange. The company was founded in 1985 by Richard Olsen, a lawyer and Oxford-educated economist who saw the practical potential of forecasting in a non-equilibrium economy. Against the common notion that currency data were just white noise, Olsen & Associates started collecting tick-by-tick foreign exchange data as early as 1986. This large and coherent database is now one of the company's major strengths.

Olsen & Associates employs thirty researchers and technicians and has placed its on-line forecasting services in some fifty banks, financial firms, and companies. The service includes real-time data on currencies as well as models that forecast their future evolution over some time horizon and supply data on the market situation. Models can be customized to meet clients' requirements in terms of time horizons, trading rules, and so on.

Dr. Olsen and co-researchers have done extensive work on the statistical behavior of currencies and on the theory of the market's functioning. Critical of the efficient market hypothesis, Dr. Olsen believes markets have their own internal structure that accounts for their not responding immediately and uniformly to external inputs. Although he regards external events as random, the market's response is predictable because of its internal structure.

Dr. Olsen sees forecasting techniques at the forefront of a radical change in the way the economy is conceived and markets organized. According to his vision, markets are not efficient and offer many possibilities for profit. Profit is the normal remuneration of the trading activity. It draws money to the markets. Acting like water in canals, profit creates liquidity to facilitate economic activity and makes the markets safer.

Olsen & Associates' forecasting models are based on the theory of financial markets they have developed and are implemented using advanced statistical techniques. The large proprietary database allows Olsen & Associates to test models with extensive out-of-sample validation. According to the company, their models achieve an average 14% return on trading credit limits and with suitable trading strategies. They are able to forecast correctly the direction of price movements of some currency couples 70% of the time, an impressive figure by any means. The company is researching neural networks and participating in a research project on genetic algorithms funded by the Swiss government.

There are also successful implementations inside financial institutions. In the U.K., TSB Bank (ex-Trustee Savings Bank) developed an application to forecast gilts for its trading subsidiary Hill Samuel Investment Management. According to Bill Edisbury, manager for emerging technologies at TSB, the neural-based system is able to predict the direction of the market with an accuracy of 65%. The goal is to arrive at a 70% accuracy rate. TSB is also experimenting with neural networks in the area of forecasting foreign exchange. They designed a hybrid system that combines traditional chartist techniques with neural networks. The objective is to predict the market's mood six months in advance, against the present capability which is in the range of a few weeks.

In the academic world, an artificial trading room (ART) has

been designed by Diethelm Wuertz and co-researchers at the Interdisciplinary Project Center (IPS) at the Swiss Federal Institute of Technology-Zurich (ETH-Z). The ART consists of three components: a database of high-frequency data, three artificial traders, and a risk-watch environment for monitoring results of the trading. Each artificial trader executes a different trading strategy based on forecasting algorithms. Trading rules are implemented in a modified time scale where time intervals are contracted or expanded in function of volatility. The risk-watch environment allows evaluation of the risk involved in taking positions. Presently, each trader implements 168 trading decisions per week for the four major currencies (German mark, Japanese yen, British pound, and Swiss franc) against the U.S. dollar. In total, over 100,000 trading decisions are executed on a yearly basis. Accessible on the World Wide Web, the quality and the pay-off of trading decisions can be observed by those interested.

The new forecasting methodologies are based on a finance theory radically different from the classical one. The methodologies will require an educational process, as was the case, for instance, when firms began to use continuous stochastic modeling. Traders and managers need to understand the meaning of indicators and the qualification of trading recommendations.

The evaluation traders make of forecasting systems varies according to experience. Kurt Kohler, foreign exchange manager at Union Bank of Switzerland's Geneva office, believes that the technology is getting more and more reliable. The strength of forecasting systems, Mr. Kohler remarks, is that they work steadily, with iron logic, producing systematic if not large benefits. He stresses, however, the need to understand the theory behind a forecasting system, an understanding that requires an investment in time. Mr. Kohler has been using the Olsen & Associates' O&A Information System for three years now.

6.3 Financial engineering

Designing securities with the appropriate attributes for trading is a financial engineering problem. Financial engineering is an engineering problem in its own right. It starts with the functional specification of a product and ends with its design specification. In between, there is a process of exploration of different options and of optimization. One of the objectives of research at Morgan Stanley is to make this process quicker and to allow financial engineers to explore more options and perform optimizations. Researchers at the firm use artificial intelligence techniques to implement the searching process of financial engineering.

Rod Beckstroem, founder of the financial engineering company C*ATS, sees the process as equivalent to mechanical computer-aided design (CAD). In mechanical CAD, designers give shape to parts and assemble them together in a virtual design, testing them numerically through procedures such as structural analysis to simulate the physical behavior of the parts. The process is repeated until the optimal solution is found.

Using financial CAD, a derivative product is created, tested, optimized for its risk/return profile, and a contract engineered. This might imply running several simulations to find the most appropriate parameters, or letting some optimization procedure do the job. Mr. Beckstroem believes that object-oriented techniques are the major enabling factor, because derivatives can be represented as networks of objects. The process of creating a derivative is thus one of assembling objects.

Financial CAD is an area where adaptive methodologies could play a fundamental role. In most engineering sectors, there is a strong push to make the process of engineering more automatic. This is proving to be an interesting field of application for adaptive methodologies. There are reasons for this. Engineering is an intrinsically adaptive process: it proceeds through loops that come ever closer to an optimal solution. In addition, engineering is not done in a void but starts from past experience. Adaptive methods have proven helpful in sectors such as numerical optimization, case-based learning, and automatic idealization. Financial CAD might profit from many of the methodologies developed in other fields to automate the engineering process.

References

Baestaens, D.-E., W. van den Bergh and D. Wood, *Neural Network Solutions for Trading in Financial Markets*, Pitman Publishing, London, 1994.

Brock, H.W., J. Lakonishok and B. LeBaron, "Simple Technical Trading Rules and the Stochastic Properties of Stock Returns," *Journal of Finance*, 47, No. 5: 1731-1764, 1992.

Guillaume, D.M., M.M. Dacorogna, R.R. Davé, U.A. Mueller, R.B. Olsen and O.V. Pictet, "From the Bird's Eye to the Microscope," *Discussion Paper of the O&A Research Group*, Zurich, October 1994.

Leinweber, D.J., "Nerds on Wall Street," First Quadrant, Pasadena, CA.

7. Risk Management

7.1 The business problem

At the moment this book is being written, risk management is a subject of high interest. A number of companies and financial institutions have suffered losses due to the use of derivative financial securities, the aim of which was precisely to control risk. Financial firms face growing risks for a number of reasons. Portfolio managers might include highly risky derivative products in their portfolios while financial firms might sell risky products in engineering complex financial deals.

There are technical and management aspects involved. The latter deal essentially with how risk is communicated to management, the management structure that controls the risk flow, and how decisions about risk are made. The technical aspects deal with how risk is evaluated and how risk control strategies are engineered.

Inside financial institutions, there is the perception of a shift in the notion of risk. Risk has become more quantitative and requires adequate computational techniques. Methodologies of risk management are presently at the center of the attention of the financial community. J.P. Morgan made public its risk management system, RiskMetrics, in an attempt to establish it as a benchmark. Most other large financial firms have similar methodologies in place. Charles Goodhart of the London School of Economics notes that many financial firms are now using their economists better: rather than ask them to predict the future, firms are directing economists' activities to ascertaining optimal risk control mechanisms.

Most persons we talked to, however, voiced some uneasiness about current techniques for measuring and controlling risk. Suran Goonatilake, researcher at University College London's department of computer science, remarks that there is risk in all financial modeling. The problem, he says, is to properly understand risk in statistical terms and to produce models validated through rigorous statistical methods. Paul Refenes, senior research fellow at the London Business School's department of decision science, adds that risk is a question of defining the business problem. Often, he remarks, miscalculations of risk arise because objectives are set in such a way that the optimization of some quantities inherently produces risk as a fall-out.

At the Swiss Federal Institute of Technology-Zurich (ETH-Z), Paul Embrechts, professor of applied probability and insurance mathematics, stresses the need for sound statistical analysis in risk management. He considers that linear statistical techniques have not exhausted their capability and advocates more research on techniques, linear and non-linear, in an attempt to understand which performs best, where, and why. The department of mathematics at ETH-Z, together with Switzerland's three largest banks, Credit Suisse, Swiss Bank Corporation, and Union Bank of Switzerland, recently founded Risklab, a research collaboration for precompetitive research in risk management.

7.2 Evaluating risk

Any firm holding a portfolio of securities is exposed to risk due to potential changes in the value of the portfolio contingent on events. There is a spectrum of contingent events that might negatively affect the value of a portfolio. A discussion paper co-authored by H. Dahl, A. Meeraus, and S. Zenios, and published by the Wharton School of Economics, divides risk into several categories: market, sector, shape, volatility, currency, credit, liquidity, and residual risk. A risk management procedure must be able to understand and quantify the size and direction of changes of each type of risk.

Market risk has different interpretations according to the market being analyzed. It is basically the rate of change with respect to factors that affect the entire market. Sector risk is the risk relative to a particular group of securities. Shape risk is applicable to the fixed-income market. It is the risk consequent to non-parallel shifts in the curve of interest rates. Volatility risk is typical of options as it is the sensitivity with respect to the volatility of securities. Currency risk is related to adverse changes in currency rates, credit risk to possible changes in credit ratings or outright defaults, and liquidity risk to the size of the bid-ask spread of securities. Lastly, residual risk includes all other risks.

The problem is that of quantifying these risks and their correlations. There are two basic approaches: analytical and simulation. The analytical approach computes risk mathematically. Instrumental to the analytical approach is the ability to represent mathematically the time evolution of risk determinants. Assuming suitable representations of the fundamental risk determinants, all other quantities are determined analytically.

The above is not a trivial task. It involves nothing less than a global finance theory. Computing market risk, for instance, assumes a suitable theory for capital asset pricing. Computing shape risk implies a theory of interest rates. Values of derivatives are sensitive, in a mathematically complex way, to a number of parameters, from volatilities of underlying securities to interest rates. The analytical approach to risk management for derivatives includes the computation of parameters — *deltas, gammas, rhos, vegas* — that express a derivative's sensitivity to a number of factors.

In principle, the analytical approach to risk management

implies the ability to describe mathematically the evolution of all financial quantities and to express mathematically their relationships. It is generally performed assuming a classical framework of efficient markets. To make the exercise mathematically tractable, a number of restrictive hypotheses are made. In most cases, Gaussian distributions are assumed so that variances and covariances fully characterize distributions.

As remarked above, many academics and practitioners voiced concerns about the validity of analytical estimates. The need for a better evaluation of distributions was widely cited as a technological must. In particular, the ability to consider non-Gaussian "fat tails" is considered important. The weight of distribution tails is a measure of the likelihood of extreme events. It is therefore an important parameter for risk evaluation.

Risk is computed at fixed time intervals, generally once a day. The evolution of risk in between evaluations can, however, be important. Michel Dacorogna, head of research at Olsen & Associates, remarks that banks run an intra-day risk that might be considerably higher than the end-of-day estimates, especially in view of non-Gaussian distributions. Northwestern University professor of finance Tim Bollerslev thinks that, by giving a better idea of tail behavior, high-frequency data might improve our knowledge of risk exposure.

To overcome the drawbacks of the analytical approach, financial firms are increasingly making use of simulation procedures. The simulation approach computes a large number of possible scenarios, eventually under extreme conditions, and evaluates the risk of global positions. Simulation is based on computing a large number of possible scenarios or paths of the evolution of risky factors without assumptions on its specific analytical form.

The recommendations of the G-30 and of the Basle Committee implicitly endorse simulation when recommending stress analysis as a sound way of performing risk management. In view of recent losses incurred by many firms, the two committees recommend that risk analysis be done under extreme scenarios. Although possible, this is analytically complex.

Simulation is computationally intensive. It has become feasible only in the last few years, with the availability of low-cost high-performance computing. Simulation is a trade-off between information and mathematical conciseness. It trades in the advantages of performing powerful deductions of analytical formulations in favor of a vast gain in information. The computational requirements of financial simulations might, however, exceed the computing power presently available. Strategies for reducing the number of simulations required include forecasting and the clustering of simulation paths.

7.3 Risk management engineering

Evaluating risk is only part of the problem of risk management; risk must also be appropriately covered. Covering risk implies a technology of financial engineering to construct appropriate portfolios and, more recently, to engineer synthetic securities. Ultimately, risk management is based on the ability to buy and sell the appropriate risk. Within the classical framework in which risk management is engineered, risk attributes are coherently priced by the market so that, in equilibrium, any risk factor is fairly priced. Covering risk, or hedging, is performed by buying and selling risk attributes that together offer the desired risk profile.

There are two intertwined problems in risk management: 1) the technological problem of engineering hedging strategies, and 2) the problem of the availability of the desired risk coverage. Hedging strategies have to be engineered to create a portfolio of securities as close as possible to the desired risk profile. The requisite attributes might not be traded so they have to be constructed synthetically. This process might in turn create additional risks, among them liquidity risk.

A major Wall Street firm underlined the liquidity risk in connection with derivative products that are basically not tradeable. Several practitioners pointed to the shortcomings inherent in the nature of transactions. Andrew E. Johnson, quantitative analyst at SBC Warburg Securities in London, points out that exotic derivatives cannot be considered liquid assets: once sold, they are not readily tradeable. The implication is that hedging has introduced a new, unwanted risk.

The problem of engineering risk management strategies is presently handled at several levels of automation. Most companies use analytical tools integrated into risk management procedures. Tools span a variety of implementations, from multifactor models to tools to compute *deltas*, *vegas*, *gammas*, and other relatively simple parametric evaluations. Clearly the importance of risk management is not the same for companies that take conservative positions in low-risk investments and firms actively engaged in buying and selling exotic securities or money managers who hold risky portfolios of derivatives.

Using the above techniques, it is possible to hedge creating portfolios that include risk in such proportions as to be nearly risk-neutral. This approach has been criticized on several grounds: it underestimates risk due to gross approximations in the distributions and allows only local risk hedges. Using parameters such as *deltas*, a manager might hedge a portfolio at a given moment but risk factors change and the hedge no longer holds. Portfolios need to be rebalanced frequently, incurring high transaction costs. Ultimately, risk might go undetected.

Ron Dembo, former professor at Yale and founder of Algorithmics, is critical of hedging approaches based on *deltas*, *vegas*, and other security sensitivities. Algorithmics has developed an alternative approach using stochastic optimization that allows one to create long-term hedges. Dr. Dembo believes that the flagship product RiskWatch has a definite advantage over classical approaches, as it does not suffer from the problem of locality of hedges.

A number of academics and practitioners believe that, ultimately, simulation is the only way to perform risk management. Atlantic Portfolio Analytics & Management bases its portfolio management on simulation. According to research director Alp Kerestecioglu, the Orlando, Florida-based investment firm wants all uncertainties "upfront." This view is shared to some extent by others. First Quadrant's head of research David Leinweber believes that the role of simulation in measuring risk is growing. He notes that standard deviations of returns are computationally tractable but don't really capture risk as it is perceived by most investors. Dr. Leinweber thinks that Monte Carlo simulations might be a better way to evaluate complex strategies.

Although present techniques do not rely on forecasting, hedging techniques do, in practice, depend on the market. Hedging works for two reasons: first, because there are business needs that allow the trading of risk attributes suitable for hedging. Hedging against exchange rate movements, for instance, is a business need on both sides of the transaction. Second, hedging is based on the willingness of investors to buy risk at a price. A company might not be willing to bear risk related to interest rates, but an investor might, betting on specific market movements. Ultimately, the marketability of risk hinges on forecasting specific price movements. In this area, forecasting methodologies will be beneficial to risk management.

Reference

Dahl, H., A. Meeraus and S.A. Zenios, "Some Financial Opti-
mization Models: Risk Management and Financial Engineer-
ing," *Fishman-Davidson Discussion Paper*, No. 50, Wharton
School of Economics, December 1989. Included in *Financial
Optimization*, edited by S. Zenios, Cambridge University
Press, Cambridge, 1993.

8. THE OUTLOOK FOR ADAPTIVE METHODS IN FINANCE

Adaptive methods hold the promise of largely expanding financial modeling. There is a broad spectrum of applications of adaptive methods both within the classical framework of efficient markets and within the new dynamic non-equilibrium framework. Within the classical framework, adaptive methods have gained a firm place as optimization devices and as estimators of parameters and functions where they provide powerful tools inside a firm theory. Examples include applications for forecasting volatility with ARCH- and GARCH-type methods as, for instance, the multifactor models developed by software house BARRA. Neural networks and other approximation schemes have potential as estimators of solutions of differential equations. An example is research at Banca Commerciale Italiana to use neural networks as estimators of the solutions of Black-Scholes differential equations.

Optimization methodologies implemented through adaptive statistical methods such as genetic algorithms are conquering new sectors of applications. These methodologies are presently being used to optimize entire algorithms as, for instance, multifactor models. First Quadrant offers an example of a financial firm that is making use of genetic algorithms to evolve its modeling.

The use of intelligent adaptive techniques is also beginning to be felt in the domain of risk management. Academics remarked that to put risk management on firmer ground, more faithful probability distributions are needed.

With the diffusion of risk management methods based on simulation, a new application domain for adaptive methods has appeared. As risk management requires the exploration of a very large set of simulated paths, computations might become inordinately complex and time-consuming. Adaptive intelligent methods are being used to constrain the space of search, reducing computing time and costs. Prof. LeBaron cites the need of coupling forecasting methods with simulation to narrow down the number of scenarios necessary to simulate. At Banca Commerciale Italiana, research is under way to reduce the simulations required by clustering simulation paths using Kohonen neural networks.

The industry's assessment of advanced computational methods within the classical framework is positive; results are generally satisfactory. The use of adaptive methods as estimators and approximators within a firm theoretical framework is growing.

Within a dynamic non-equilibrium framework, a more cautious evaluation is necessary. Academic research has made ample use of adaptive methods to explain new stylized facts discovered through the analysis of the large quantities of data presently available. This approach has been successful, producing important results such as the ARCH and GARCH methods. However, most academics feel that adaptive methods need the firmer ground of comprehensive theoretical formulations. As remarked by Prof. Bollerslev, the developer of GARCH, it is time to go beyond adaptive methods and to produce more theory. Cornell University's Maureen O'Hara concurs, noting that a structural explanation of market microstructure is now necessary.

The present generation of financial modeling is only a first approximation, as it relies on a number of simplifying assumptions. The next generation of financial modeling will adopt more realistic assumptions and will model the dynamic, non-equilibrium behavior of the economy. This new generation of tools will recognize that markets have an intrinsic structure and will explicitly include this structure in the theory. While traders presently exploit market "anomalies," future decision-support and automatic trading systems will capture the full dynamics of the market. Developing this new generation of modeling will, however, require some firm theoretical foundation.

Presently, and from the practical side, the use of adaptive methods in the new non-equilibrium framework is related principally to forecasting. Efficient markets set an upper bound to forecastability as expressed by the risk/return relationship. However, the new framework questions the efficient market hypothesis (EMH) and opens the door to forecasting price movements, making excess returns theoretically possible. Academics generally feel that, while forecasting is quite difficult as markets are close to efficiency, it can, nevertheless, be industrially profitable.

The global impact of automatic forecasting methodologies today is, however, marginal. Matt Ridley, author of *The Economist*'s 1993 special "The Mathematics of Markets" estimates that these technologies have achieved only 5% of their potential in financial applications. But he adds, "They've only just arrived."

There are two considerations to be made, acceptance and performance. Acceptance of forecasting technologies among analysts and traders is still low. "When traders hear of computer technology," says a proprietary FX trader at a major European bank, "they imagine their jobs disappearing."

Presently, the best computerized forecasting methods and decision-support systems are improving on the capabilities of previously used techniques and have reached a level of performance comparable to that of the best traders. They can already enhance the average performance of traders and extend their ability to cover a broader market sector.

The assessment made by Morgan Stanley reflects, by and large, Wall Street's evaluation of these technologies. According to the firm's head of artificial intelligence, Kevin Holley, profitable forecasting is possible as shown by the fact that traders forecast in their daily activity; without the possibility of forecasting, a trader's activity would not be profitable. In the present state-of-the-art, the best human traders — combining hunch, information, and theory — perform better than automated approaches. This comparatively low performance level removes a major business incentive for implementing these technologies on a large scale. However, the company believes that forecasting methodologies can improve the bottom line by reducing operational costs and enhancing the average ability of traders to work profitably in a broader market sector. At the same time, there is the expectation that performance will greatly improve with the maturing of the technology.

Hasanat Dewan, vice president and head of the database project at Morgan Stanley, says that today's technology is still immature. Adaptive methods work well on simple patterns but there are many unresolved problems when dealing with complex patterns. He believes that there are major theoretical deficiencies, as the process of generalization is not well-understood. In addition, Dr. Dewan cites a basic lack of data, given that most firms have not collected tick-by-tick data in usable format in the past years. Creating an adequate database is a major challenge.

Other major Wall Street firms with substantial technical prowess have made similar evaluations. Erik Carlson, director of strategic analytics and research at Prudential Securities, believes that there is forecastability in the markets and that this forecastability will eventually be exploited scientifically. He believes, however, that the effort presently required is too large to provide any benefits to business.

The new forecasting methods are introducing a type of risk that is difficult to evaluate, as there is no theory to explain it. Citibank's Dan Schutzer, director of new technologies, remarks that although computerized forecasting can show positive results in a statistically meaningful way, the risk that it might generate substantial local losses is high. He points out that demonstrating that an adaptive methodology such as neural networks offers statistically meaningful forecasts is not sufficient if the global risk profile of the procedure is not known.

The risk of local losses is a critical point raised by a number of interviewees. Citibank's Dr. Schutzer, for instance, says that the bank's essentially negative evaluation of their experience in neural-based forecasting is due precisely to the problem of local losses. Forecasting algorithms might make money, but occasionally they might lose lots more. The absence of a framework for evaluating the risk/return profile of forecast-based investments creates a problem for management.

In summary, it is fair to say that industry makes a two-sided assessment of computer-based forecasting techniques in finance. On one hand, the technologies have had only marginal impact to date and are considered immature. On the other hand, a number of pioneering efforts are showing consistently good results. There is the expectation, among researchers and practitioners alike, that we are witnessing the beginning of a revolution in the handling of finance.

PART III
ISSUES AND THE MARKET

9. THE MARKET FOR PRODUCTS AND SERVICES

Previous chapters outlined the major applications for simulation and adaptive technologies in finance. This chapter looks at how this translates into a market for hardware, software, and services. It starts with a global assessment of the market's evolution, goes on to explore the question of the development of a commercial software and service industry and the structuring of applications, and closes examining the role of government and public research.

9.1 The market as seen by hardware vendors

According to Ben C. Barnes, vice president for marketing, development, and strategy at IBM's RISC System/6000 Division, behind the development of the scientific information technology in finance, is an increase in the use of and capabilities of financial modeling. Mr. Barnes sees an important transformation in finance as modeling capabilities benefit from the accumulation of past data. Data — the accumulation and analysis of large amounts of transaction data — are the key to the development of the financial scientific information technology market. Unlike in the past, when transaction data were used mainly for accounting and similar purposes, in the future, data will be used to scientifically engineer financial products.

Cray Research, the company that created the market for supercomputers in the 1970s, is focused on the financial modeling sector. Charles Finan, formerly a researcher at the Los

Alamos National Laboratory and now director of financial modeling at Cray, feels that the evolution of financial modeling is following lines parallel to that of scientific computing in research and manufacturing in the 1970s and 1980s. Cray has seen large financial firms hire hundreds of scientists and build teams similar to those existing in the national laboratories or in large manufacturing companies. Dr. Finan believes this structure is here to stay.

Cray Research finds that the demands of scientists working in finance are similar to those of physical scientists: efficient, cost-effective, number-crunching machines, and system support in tasks such as tuning algorithms or designing basic software. Large financial firms now have an R&D structure similar to that of large manufacturing companies.

In Europe, where the environment is less competitive and the flow of financial transactions smaller, the perspective of a company like Siemens-Nixdorf is influenced by the need to overcome barriers to advanced scientific technologies. In introducing its neural network environment SENN, the Munich-based company formed a consortium of financial institutions to define requirements and share experience.

In designing the map of the evolution of the market for scientific applications in finance, and in particular for adaptive methodologies, it is necessary to place this development in the context of the prevailing computational modeling methods. These are based on theoretical developments in the 1960s and the 1970s, with the formalization of general-equilibrium theories. This line of development has not run out of steam, and there are important advances in the pipeline. New methodologies based on an adaptive data-rich approach will have to coexist with and be integrated into the existing technologies, creating, perhaps, a new theoretical synthesis.

9.2 The shaping up of a software and service industry

If experience from other sectors is a guide, banking and finance will see the development of a commercial software offering. In nearly every sector in science and technology, e.g., aerospace, automotive, and chemical, with the maturing of technology commercial software was developed and became the preferred choice of companies and research centers alike. Even in as highly a competitive sector as pharmaceuticals, companies prefer, when possible, to adopt off-the-shelf software tools for designing drugs, concentrating their efforts on the specific issues of their discipline.

The development of a software and service industry is not without obstacles. Some markets have proved to be too small and/or too difficult to sustain development efforts. In fluid dynamics, for example, high-end applications are still implemented as proprietary software: the market potential is too small to attract software developers.

The majority of scientific applications are, however, now implemented as commercial software in sectors as diverse as structural analysis, computational chemistry, computational biology, and electronic circuit design. In only a limited number of sectors is ownership of proprietary software tools considered a competitive advantage. In most cases, the competitive advantage comes from domain-specific knowledge, not from the tools.

There are a number of reasons for this. First, the cost of proprietary software development and maintenance might rapidly become prohibitive. A team working in isolation rapidly runs out of scientific steam unless a major effort is made to attract new talents and to keep development going. This effort is very expensive. Laboratories working on military technologies have certainly produced a stream of new proprietary software, but the size of the endeavor was gigantic, involving thousands of experienced scientists. Many firms interviewed for this book, including some of the largest, stated that the growing cost of software development is a major management concern.

Second, it is difficult to maintain a competitive advantage over time. The mere knowledge that a development is possible generally leads to a race to reproduce the development. While it is possible to hide technological achievements for a long time in the military sector, it is rarely possible to do so in business. Quite the contrary, advantages need to be publicized. As a result, proprietary software technologies typically offer a competitive advantage for awhile, but competition catches up rapidly. At this point, it becomes advantageous to use standard software. Many financial firms are now more open than in the past about their development efforts and seem willing to share, at least to some extent, their experience with other players.

In addition, commercial software is frequently better engineered than in-house products, and it can benefit from a broad variety of experience.

These factors point to the likely successful evolution of a commercial offering of scientific software for the financial sector. IBM's Ben Barnes identified the shaping up of a commercial software offering as a key step in the evolution of the market. In his opinion, falling hardware prices and the consequent expansion of the market will attract software developers. Availability of products will fuel additional demand and foster new development, creating a positive upward spiral of investment and development.

There are, however, obstacles. Software developers need to work in close cooperation with users to engineer products with the requisite features. This was the case, for instance, in the development of neural-based card-related fraud detection software in the retail banking sector. Software developers created partnerships with their clients to acquire the data necessary to train the networks and to understand what features the product should offer. The development of financial software such as modeling software will have an even greater need for cooperation. From the point of view of a commercial enterprise, however, the need to form partnerships could be dissuasive. Joint efforts are difficult to engineer and limit the profitability of the activity.

Another obstacle commercial developers will have to face is represented by the investment financial firms have already made in software and the size of teams they have pulled together. Any commercial package must be able to be integrated into existing software structures, a technical and marketing hurdle. In addition, large in-house teams are unlikely to welcome a massive introduction of third-party software.

A commitment to in-house development is also an obstacle. Many major firms simply prefer to develop software internally. For some, as Pasadena, California-based Countrywide Funding, the largest U.S. originator of mortgages, building their tools internally to create a competitive edge is part of the corporate culture. Others, like Morgan Stanley, believe that the challenge of rapidly changing internal needs are unlikely to be met by external suppliers.

Some interviewees noted that while the largest financial institutions may prefer in-house development, smaller firms do not have the resources to sustain proprietary development, and turn to commercially available software. If, however, one looks at the market for scientific software, one finds that it typically responds to specific needs and is used by a wide range of companies. The structural analysis software used by Boeing in designing airplanes and by Ford in designing cars is used by companies large and small in designing mechanical parts. The same specialized software for crash analysis is used to test the crash worthiness of cars, mold ordinary metal pieces, and design aluminum pop cans. To capture the market, software developers will have to offer products that satisfy the needs of players large and small alike.

It is legitimate to ask to what extent the preference for in-house development is driven by the absence of a sufficiently strong commercial offering. Competing, however, with big internal teams might require an amount of investment that will prove discouraging for many firms. Rod Beckstroem, founder of the capital markets software firm C*ATS, remarks that their investment in software development is in the range of $30mn and growing.

Despite some difficulties, it is likely that a commercial software offering for scientific banking and financial applications will develop. There is already a strong commercial offering in areas such as business problem modeling and optimization with companies like Quantum Development and Right Information Systems; financial engineering with companies like C*ATS, Infinity, Renaissance, and SunGard; portfolio management with companies like BARRA in the U.S. and FSTD in the U.K.; derivatives pricing with companies like A-J Financial Systems and FEA; and in the risk management sector with companies like Algorithmics, GAT, and Kamakura.

Off-the-shelf software is not the only component of the developing scientific financial offering. Companies providing customized applications or packaged services might also play an important role. In the area of customized software, entrepreneurial academics and researchers have started companies, often as the commercial development of research conducted at university or in research centers. The strength of these start-ups is the ability to tackle pointed problems at the cutting edge of technology.

Tica Technologies in Cambridge, Massachusetts designs applications based on adaptive methods. Its founder Lawrence Davis is a leading researcher in the field of genetic algorithms.

The company applies adaptive technologies in a number of areas, including finance. Among its clients are the U.S. Navy and Wall Street traders. Dr. Lawrence benefits from informal links with scientists at the nearby Massachusetts Institute of Technology.

Also in Cambridge, Foundation Technologies provides customized software and consultancy based on artificial intelligence and neural networks. Founder Tod Loofbourrow teaches artificial intelligence at Harvard University. The company was among the first software developers applying neural network techniques to the financial markets.

London-based SearchSpace was founded by academics including Suran Goonatilake and Jason Kingdon from the computer science department of University College London. Search-Space provides customized solutions based on advanced statistics and intelligent systems, applying the technologies to solve problems in areas like marketing, fraud detection, and financial forecasting and trading. SearchSpace created the pilot study to detect insider trading for the London Stock Exchange. The system uses a combination of adaptive methods, including neural networks, fuzzy logic, and genetic algorithms.

The third component of the scientific software offering is represented by companies supplying a complete packaged service. In trading, two service companies have pioneered computer-based forecasting techniques, The Prediction Company in Santa Fe, New Mexico and Olsen & Associates in Zurich. Their strategies, however, are different.

The Prediction Company works under a near exclusive contract initially signed with the Chicago-based securities firm O'Connor & Associates and subsequently transferred to Swiss Bank Corporation when they bought O'Connor. The Prediction Company provides a complete forecasting service based on proprietary technology; Swiss Bank Corporation funds the trading.

Olsen & Associates provides a fee-based on-line information and forecasting service for foreign exchange and futures. Companies like Olsen & Associates play an important role in enabling financial institutions and corporate treasuries to acquire a first-class decision-support system, avoiding the lengthy process of building one from scratch.

9.3 The structure of the commercial offering

There are many questions related to the shape of the market and how it will progress towards offering increased functionalities.

According to Ben Barnes at IBM's RISC System/6000 Division, ease of use will be a major consideration for the development of a commercial software offering. Joseph Elad, founder of Quantum Development, foresees the widespread embedding of problem-solving methodologies to enhance user friendliness. The company's product Quantum Leap brings scientific methods close to the user with problem-solving methodologies that help to define problems and automatically choose the best computational method(s) for solving them.

Ease of use is not only a question of legible presentation and easy commands, but involves the question of automating intelligent tasks. For the business user, a methodology is easy to use when it is close to the business problem to be solved and frees the user from computational considerations. The scientific user has a similar attitude. It is this attitude that was responsible for the development of the current generation of scientific software that shields users from problems unrelated to the specific scientific or engineering problem under examination.

When application software eliminates one layer of competencies or saves on expensive tasks, its appeal grows. In many cases, the competency or time required to run the application is a blocking factor for its development. Users might decide to run an application only when automatic procedures become available. In the scientific world, there are many such examples. The problem of creating discretization for structural analysis applications, for example, was so time-consuming that many potential users refrained from adopting the methodology. The subsequent development of automatic meshing extended the list of potential users.

Tica Technologies' Dr. Davis remarks that genetic algorithms will find broad applications only when the user will not have to worry about programming them. He regards software such as Evolver, a package from Axcelis that combines the Excel spreadsheet with genetic algorithms, an important step in this direction, because the user only has to worry about entering the data. The package does the rest.

Software like Quantum Leap goes one step further. It allows users to run optimization applications without any knowledge of the mathematics of optimization software and with limited expertise in modeling business problems. It uses problem-solving methodologies to set up a dialogue with the user and to search for the best algorithm for solving the current problem. In doing so, Quantum Leap frees the user from considerations on optimization technology, thereby extending optimization software to a potentially large user base.

Many interviewees remarked that technologies such as neural networks make users feel uneasy because they behave as a "black box," giving answers but no explanations. It should, however, be remarked that the diffusion of computational techniques has always required that additional functions be taken as black boxes. The key point is to characterize black boxes in functional terms with sufficient precision. In other words, users do not need to know how functions are performed as long as they feel comfortable with the specification and the limits of validity of functions. This stage has not yet been reached with adaptive methods in financial applications.

At any stage in the development of computational science in a given discipline, there are a number of functions that are taken as black boxes. Global functions can be represented as a network of black boxes, each performing a number of functions. During a phase of progress and discovery, both the components and the networks become questionable, and any new application is developed taking into consideration a large number of details. With the maturing of the technology, new black boxes and a new network of functional relationships are defined. In the new stage, black boxes are well-defined from a functional point of view and the limits of their applicability clearly identified.

Consider, for example, the development of structural analysis. In the first stages of development of the technology, the only available black boxes were the analysis of simple component structures, while the analysis of a complex structure had to be performed under user control. In most cases, it is now possible to perform automatically the analysis of an entire structure. The structure itself is designed by a computer-aided design procedure. The whole process of creating and refining discretizations and running the analysis has become automatic. In addition, the limits of the process are known. The new black box is the entire process of analysis. The next step is to perform the entire optimization of a structure as a black box, without additional manual intervention.

In financial analytics, standard methods have reached the stage of black box. To determine the price of a complex derivative, a trader simply runs the program with a single command and, if sufficient computing power is available, he gets an answer in a few seconds. The whole process is transparent; the trader knows the limits of validity of the answer he gets.

The next step will be to extend the same approach to functions as forecasting, with the use of methods such as neural networks. Presently this approach is still questionable, as there is no general agreement about the limits of validity of the process. The previous chapters explored different experiences and points of view. It is, however, only a question of time before a forecasting approach can be made fully automatic.

In conclusion, scientific methodologies will become widespread in the financial sector as they become more user friendly, which essentially means more automatic. There are already a number of applications that have reached, or are approaching, this stage. Optimization is one such example.

Another question is whether the market will prefer solutions or building blocks, the type of software that IBM calls "middleware." Most scientific markets essentially saw the development of scientific middleware while business software developed both. Even today, after some 40 years of development in mechanical engineering, there is basically no complete, domain-specific, engineering application software, while there are many complete business applications.

According to IBM's Ben Barnes, the development of middleware will be fundamental for the growth of the financial scientific software market. Many large firms concur, on the condition that commercial application software must integrate into existing environments and, by necessity, be made of customizable modules. Because object-oriented techniques allow the creation of modules that can be used independently, they are seen by many as a key technology.

9.4 Role of government-funded initiatives and research

Many scientific applications used in industry today are the result of some government investment, often in the defense sector. The role of major laboratories and of large universities in developing new scientific software should not be underestimated. These institutions must be credited with having opened the door to scientific software and accelerating the engineering of science that has made its way into manufacturing.

It is more difficult for scientific financial software to profit from similar research. In the U.S., a number of initiatives jointly funded by the government and by private firms are now shaping up. At Syracuse University, the Northeast Parallel Architectures Center (NPAC) is providing technology transfer to companies that might benefit from high-performance computing and communication technologies. Miloje Makivic heads a group that works at applying parallel, distributed, and World Wide Web computing technologies to financial applications. The group developed a path-integral Monte Carlo method for the valuation of derivative securities. The center is also developing applications in global optimization with simulated annealing for large-scale asset management applications. According to Dr. Makivic, the research objective is to apply the techniques of statistical mechanics to modeling the non-equilibrium behavior of the market. NPAC recently joined the Financial Services Technology Consortium (FSTC).

The FSTC grew out of a research agreement between Citibank and the Lawrence Livermore National Laboratories. The director of new technologies at Citibank, Dan Schutzer, saw the potential of a large-scale research cooperation and promoted the expansion of the initiative. The FSTC now includes some of the major U.S. government-funded laboratories (Lawrence Livermore, Los Alamos, Oak Ridge, Sandia, FermiLab), major U.S. banks (including Bank of America, Chase Manhattan Bank, Citibank, Wells Fargo), university research centers (including NPAC at Syracuse University), and suppliers of information technology. The FSTC is a step in the direction of using large research facilities for finance.

In the U.S., financial firms have taken advantage of the availability of scientists with the type of skills needed. Often these scientists came from large universities or national laboratories where they had accumulated years of experience on non-linear computational methods. Researchers and professors have also founded consulting companies that play a role in providing financial firms with the necessary skills.

In Europe, the situation is somewhat different. There are a number of academic initiatives, led by leading economists or by academics who saw the possibility of applying advanced computational techniques. In the U.K., the Department of Trade and Industry sponsored technology transfer programs with the objective of introducing adaptive technologies, and in particular neural network technologies, into sectors such as retail banking and finance. The European Community provided funding to a number of projects in the area of neural networks with the Hansa project, and genetic algorithms with the Papagena project. Hansa is aimed at creating a family of utilities for decision-support systems, Papagena at creating a parallel environment for genetic algorithms.

10. TECHNOLOGY ISSUES

A number of issues of importance to those deciding on, planning, or implementing adaptive methods emerged from the field research. They have been grouped into technical and management issues. The technical issues include the availability of data, questions on theory and methods, user friendliness, and computing power. The management issues include championing technology, defining the business problem, building teams, in-house development and commercially available software and services, and considerations on the global context.

10.1 Availability of data

The critical role of data was widely cited. In many cases, interviewees attributed the success or failure of an application to the amount and quality of data available. While the problem of data is by and large technique-independent, University College London researcher Suran Goonatilake remarks that adaptive methods, and neural networks in particular, are more "data hungry" than traditional methods.

Availability of data is crucial in both model building and model validation. In the model building phase, a large amount of data is needed to train complex models. In validation, a large amount of data is important for ensuring the proper testing of models using rigorous out-of-sample validation techniques. The importance of out-of-sample validation can hardly be overemphasized. Data are also crucial for theory formulation, to support scientists searching for laws with a high level of explanatory power.

Even more critical than the quantity of data is their quality. This includes their accuracy and consistency, the conditions of sampling, and so on. Data must be significant to the problem under consideration, otherwise they become irrelevant. Many firms that have abundant data still find that extensive preprocessing is needed to make the data significant to the problem.

The problem of data is particularly acute in the trading area, as financial time series, complex in themselves, show very complex behavior. Morgan Stanley has launched a major internal project for building and analyzing large databases. The Prediction Company, which builds computer-based forecasting models for trading futures, considers data one of their top priorities. The success of Zurich-based Olsen & Associates in building forecasting models for foreign exchange markets is due, in part, to the database of high-frequency data they have been building since 1986.

While the need for data is generally recognized, the amount of data required depends on the phenomena to be modeled and the methodologies used. Highly general models able to capture global features, taking into consideration economic fundamentals, might require very long series of data. Aamir Sheikh, formerly an economics professor at Indiana University and now a senior consultant at BARRA, believes that forecasting expected returns in the stock market might require upwards of 30 years of data to capture all the fundamentals of the problem. He notes that the longest time series available date back to the 1920s-1930s.

For approaches that concentrate on short-term forecasts, e.g., in highly liquid markets such as the foreign exchange market, shorter time series might be sufficient. John Moody, associate professor of computer science at the Oregon Graduate Institute, believes that one key to forecasting with adaptive methods is the ability to build accurate models from relatively short series of data. The reason, he explains, is that we will increasingly find that old data is less and less relevant: with the diffusion of sophisticated modeling techniques, markets evolve faster, trend less, and exhibit increasing choppiness.

The need for data has one important consequence: inherently complex, projects using adaptive methods must gain management attention in the early phase of development. Proof-of-the-concept projects are likely to fail if there is a mismatch between the complexity of the problem and the amount of data available. Many projects have failed because the need for good, coherent data was underestimated. Results were consequently inconsistent or disappointing, and projects were cancelled or downgraded on the basis of poor technical performance. A problem of project management might then be taken as a failure of the technology.

The availability of data should be one of the first management concerns when planning projects based on adaptive methods. If data are not available in the amount required by a project, management should consider ways to address the problem before starting to experiment.

The need for data also puts serious constraints on academic research. Academia rarely has the resources necessary to build the appropriate databases for these applications. In many cases, researchers are addressing the problem working together with the industry. The NeuroForecasting Club in London is one such example. More recently, Olsen & Associates offered to make available to academics their database of over 20 million bid-ask FX quotes collected since 1986. This initiative will change the outlook of academic research by enabling new studies using high-frequency data.

10.2 Theory and methods

In making decisions on adaptive methods, management makes a conceptual commitment. It is not simply a question of the choice of a product or a tool but the choice of a way of doing business. Common in the high-tech industry where companies are used to taking stances on questions of theory and methods, this situation is relatively new in the financial sector.

Science-averse management might feel it is safe to shy away from making a choice. In practice, this luxury does not exist. By doing nothing, management implicitly chooses the less advanced technologies, a choice that undermines the firm's future competitiveness.

In finance and trading, there is an important conceptual step regarding the ability to model and forecast financial processes. In function of some basic conceptual decision, different techniques might be chosen, with important consequences to the organization. A similar situation occurred three decades ago in manufacturing, when computer-aided design methods were first introduced. Decisions on questions of theory must be made at two levels: first at the level of economics and finance theory, second at the level of the theory underlying adaptive methods.

Theoretical questions related to finance theory will become important. Adaptive methods create local models as a first step towards a final all-encompassing theory. A global theory, able to explain the market dynamics in a non-equilibrium environment, would be highly beneficial, as it would place technology on much firmer ground, and would develop interpretative concepts. Such a theory is, however, not yet available.

Firms will have to decide if they want to adhere strictly to the classical efficient paradigm or begin to explore the realm of non-equilibrium dynamics. Local adaptive models might seem similar in the two frameworks. The interpretation of results and the conceptual connections are, however, radically different. Often, judgment of results depends on the underlying theoretical evaluation. In particular, performance judgements of forecasting are significantly affected by theoretical considerations.

Barclays' senior technology consultant, Inderjit Sandhu, notes a potential trap for practitioners. It is deceptively easy, he says, to start a project without a lot of hard thinking, only to discover later that lack of a fundamental understanding of the business problem and the technology is a blocking factor. His advice to any novice is to get first a good book on statistics, second, a good book on the theory of control, and, third, a good book on neural networks. Others, as University College London computer science researcher Suran Goonatilake, remark that the field of adaptive methodologies is theoretically more complex than many believe. A very good understanding of mathematics and statistics is, he says, necessary.

Among the theoretical issues relative to adaptive methods, there are basic questions about the validity of the generalization process. It is easy to perceive that the subject of generalization is either too difficult or too simple. It is too difficult because it is really the subject of making automatic science, of creating algorithms that make scientific discoveries automatically. Forecasting is ultimately the building of a generalized model starting from raw data, a task that can be perceived as exceedingly difficult. On the other hand, it is easy to consider the daily work on adaptive methods as a painstaking process of tuning off-the-shelf models through out-of-sample validation, with little or no theoretical contribution.

Among the theoretical considerations, validation of results has a place of its own. A major development in statistics was the introduction, in the 1970s, of out-of-sample validation. Out-of-sample validation is a procedure that requires the division of training and test data into separate classes, eventually with specific strategies such as leave-one-out or jackknifing. Out-of-sample validation offers a statistically rigorous way of testing learning algorithms and has become a major tool in the design of adaptive algorithms. Researchers tune learning algorithms through out-of-sample testing, virtually the only way to ensure that a learning algorithm can show good generalization capabilities.

Interviewees voiced concerns about the consistent application of rigorous statistical validation methods in research. Matthias Seewald, portfolio manager at Allianz Life Insurance, believes there is still too much subjectivity in basic issues related to designing and training neural networks. Allianz Life is using the Siemens-Nixdorf SENN neural network environment to forecast turning points of indicators to be used in asset allocation. Dr. Goonatilake notes that, due to pressures of various types, many adaptive models are not being properly tested. Results, therefore, might not be so reliable. As out-of-sample validation is typically time-consuming and computationally expensive, shortcuts might seem attractive. It is an important issue that needs attention.

Validation techniques are a subject for research. At the Santa Fe Institute, researcher David Wolpert has introduced "stacking," a scheme for generalization that is an extension of out-of-sample validation. Out-of-sample techniques are typically used in a winner-takes-all strategy, i.e., several generalizers are tested and the one that gets the best score is adopted. However, global scoring systems do not take into consideration that generalizers might be particularly efficient for only a portion of the data. Stacking is a technique for combining the results of different generalizers, taking the best of each.

Hybridization of different systems is another issue. According to Dr. Goonatilake, hybridization is the research agenda for the next five years. We are, he says, just beginning to understand the strengths and weaknesses of the various adaptive methodologies and the subcomponents of the problems. As we learn to apply specific technologies to the subcomponents, combining adaptive methods with traditional techniques as analytics and statistics, Dr. Goonatilake believes we have a "win-win situation."

Joseph Elad, founder of Quantum Development, cites Nobel laureate Herbert Simon of Carnegie Mellon University, who said: "We must let the problem that we are trying to solve determine the methods we apply to it instead of letting our technology determine what problems we are willing and able to tackle." Quantum Leap, the business modeling software package developed by his company, does that through a problem-solving methodology that chooses automatically and dynamically the best among 28 available methodologies.

There is agreement that among the adaptive computational methods there is no best methodology in absolute, but a set of tools that can be combined. How, exactly, is a difficult problem. There are partial solutions, but not yet a single unifying framework.

10.3 Ancillary technologies and user friendliness

The need to place adaptive methodologies in the context of man-machine interaction emerged as an important issue. This need is especially felt in the area of trading. Joseph De Feo, director of group operations and technology at Barclays Bank in London, foresees that the ability of a human to focus on problems will be severely challenged as financial instruments grow in complexity and computer models spew out information feeds at increasing speeds. According to Kevin Holley, head of artificial intelligence at Morgan Stanley, visualization and data interpretation techniques are an important part of his company's research agenda. Another major Wall Street firm says visualization gets high priority as a core competence under development. As Bill

Edisbury, manager of emerging technologies at TSB Bank, put it, "Without good presentation, good data is useless."

For suppliers of financial systems, effective presentation of data is an important consideration. Olsen & Associates has introduced a new generation of visual representations of forecasting results with the objective of making the information more suggestive for traders. Algorithmics uses an elaborate graphics system not only to display data but also to allow operators to quickly input "what if" scenarios by simply moving curves and graphs.

Visualization is one of a set of technologies for rendering the man-machine interface more effective. Carnegie Mellon University has developed the notion of the SILKy human interface, able to handle Speech, Images, Learning, and Knowledge. Among the features of intelligent interfaces now within reach are the ability to adapt to the user and to make up for missing or incomplete data. In financial applications, interfaces are part of the reasoning of the trader, so their design is not only a question of effective presentation but of reasoning about data.

Although there is wide agreement on the importance of the man-machine interface, the effective integration of interfacing technologies with financial modeling remains a challenge. Most trading systems still use rather simple presentations, such as charts and tables.

User friendliness is a major consideration in the selection of technologies and products. Robin Griffiths, chief technical analyst at James Capel, London, explains that they experimented with several off-the-shelf neural network packages; user friendliness dictated the choice.

David Leinweber, research head at First Quadrant, cites another dimension of user friendliness: the ability to implement applications through simple descriptions. Dr. Leinweber was among the first to apply this concept in the financial world, developing a system that allows users to define applications in their own language.

In planning applications, management must be attentive to the integration of machine intelligence methods in a working environment, another facet of the commitment to the technology. The widespread use of simulation in mechanical and chemical engineering, for example, is due not only to the development of supercomputers but also to the widespread use of visualization tools, including three-dimensional representation and virtual reality to make results intuitively understandable.

10.4 Computing power

The computing power required in financial applications is a subject of debate. Academics like Stavros Zenios of the Wharton School of Economics advocate the use of large computing power in finance. He points out that computing power allows for qualitative changes in financial transactions. While reducing the time of a computation from 6 to 3 hours might be of limited interest, the ability to perform pricing valuations in the lapse of a telephone call is a qualitative change in the way of doing business. In his paper *Parallel and Supercomputing in the Financial Services Industry*, Prof. Zenios cites the experience of Prudential Securities, a pioneer in the use of massively parallel machines. The New York securities firm was able to cut valuation time for pricing securities from several hours to 20 seconds, achieving the goal of giving its traders a real-time decision-support tool.

The need for large, centralized number crunchers is not universally shared. Citibank's Dan Schutzer believes that workstations are powerful enough to handle problems typically encountered in finance and in analyzing market data. He remarks that the collective computing power amassed in a trading room with hundreds of workstations might be very large indeed. The New York-based bank has both powerful parallel machines, mainly for handling large databases, and workstations for handling even demanding financial applications.

Rod Beckstroem, founder of the capital markets software firm C*ATS, believes that, in a few years, inexpensive parallel machines will be on traders' desks, allowing the interactive design of complex financial products, and performing simulations and optimizations in near real time. He believes that as forecasting methodologies become widespread, the need for computational power at the level of the trader will grow.

Cray Research's Robert Farley says the real issue is the cost effectiveness of computer solutions. Although individual workstations might be powerful enough to handle financial calculations, he believes that today's supercomputers offer a better price performance ratio with respect to large networks of workstations. With the configuration and price of supercomputers scaling downwards, Cray has installed their conventional vector machines in firms such as Merrill Lynch, Freddie Mac, and Atlantic Portfolio Analytics and Management. The company now offers a parallel machine, the T3D. At least one has been installed at a major financial firm.

At Merrill Lynch, the choice of a supercomputer architecture was driven by the need for raw computing power. The Cray Y-MP2E system is being used to price and hedge complex financial instruments.

Hans-Otto Isbert, head of Siemens-Nixdorf's Neural Network Competence Center in Frankfurt, thinks that the increasingly powerful Risc workstations essentially satisfy the computing requirements of neural-based forecasting applications. Siemens-Nixdorf supplies SENN, an internally developed neural network environment for complex analysis and forecasting. Mr. Isbert foresees, however, the need for parallel machines or specialized neuro-computers as the time lag for forecasting shortens, and he believes that real-time controlling will require supercomputing power. The company is now commercializing its Synapse 1, a neuro-computer developed in a joint research project between the Siemens-Nixdorf research lab in Munich and the University of Karlsruhe.

Ben Barnes, vice president for marketing, development, and strategy at IBM's RISC System/6000 Division, thinks that powerful parallel machines will be essential to handling the large databases that the financial institutions are building up. The financial sector is, he believes, at the beginning of a revolution characterized by the accumulation of massive quantities of data and their intelligent handling.

It is fair to say that the need for large computing power in banking and finance has been demonstrated, and that the need will grow in the future. How to supply the needed power is, however, a question of a firm's information technology strategy. In planning advanced methods in both banking and finance, management has to take a hard look at the hardware resources available and evaluate the computing needs of the applications.

11. Management Issues

11.1 Championing technology

When asked what factors determine the success of neural-based forecasting systems for trading, Andrew E. Johnson mentioned, together with discipline and patience, management backing. A quantitative analyst at SBC Warburg in London, Mr. Johnson — like Bradford Lewis at Fidelity — is using NeuralWare's Professional II neural network tools.

In case after case, our research found that management commitment was behind the successful large-scale implementation of machine-intelligence technologies. These methodologies need champions at senior level with a sufficient grasp of technology and the power to drive change through the organization. Small-scale projects will find it difficult to survive and grow. One reason for this, as already discussed above, is that these methodologies are "data hungry."

At Countrywide Funding, the largest originator of mortgages in the United States, the technology drive starts at the top. Since the company's beginning 25 years ago, the cornerstone of Countrywide's business strategy has been to use technology to develop a competitive edge. In a recent interview, vice chairman Angelo Mozilo cited technology as the single most important factor behind the company's success. Countrywide Funding provides residential mortgages to the public and transforms them into collateralized mortgage obligations (CMOs) to be sold on Wall Street. Management wants the highest level of technology, not

131

only to ensure good service to retail customers, but also to provide quality financial products for trading.

At Citicorp, chairman John Reed himself is behind the technology drive. An engineer by training, Mr. Reed sees technology as a major factor for success. Not only is Citicorp committed to technology, it is exploring unconventional ways of using science to reinvent the bank. The New York bank supports leading edge research on complex systems and the market by W. Brian Arthur at the Santa Fe Institute. It has also initiated joint research projects with America's national labs. The objective is to exploit the immense volume of data generated by electronic commerce, using machine-learning algorithms for inductive inference from large databases to be used in forecasting and financial modeling.

At the Amsterdam-based universal bank ABN-Amro, it was the bank's executive vice president and head of the directorate treasury Ted Zwierzina who got behind advanced computational methods. Today a team of technical analysts is working on converting the bank's linear statistical techniques into non-linear dynamic techniques through a process of optimization, employing neural networks and rule-based systems.

Boston-based Fidelity Investments has an open, pragmatic attitude towards technology and scientific development. Technological prowess is considered a fundamental determinant of success and scientific development an integral part of the business. Technology has management's support. A measuring system is in place to evaluate the results of new methodologies and plan their introduction.

Morgan Stanley's full-spectrum research effort has top management backing. Technology is part of the business planning process and a sector where the company is investing heavily. The company has also made a reputation for its ongoing effort to teach technology to its trading and management ranks. Managers and traders are trained regularly on "arcane" topics such as continuous stochastic processes.

In manufacturing, champions are often found in the scientific areas, where they conduct their experiments in laboratories before taking them to top management. In finance, this process must be more direct, reaching senior levels from the start. The reason is that technological changes immediately affect operations: their viability can be judged only in business terms.

The need for immediate management attention is a serious obstacle to the development of advanced computational techniques. This is especially true where senior management is not conversant in scientific disciplines. It is only in the last decade that the inner workings of financial and economic processes have become the subject of quantitative science, opening the way to technological applications of scientific theory. Understanding this change is a challenge to management. The deployment of advanced computational methodologies is not a local factor, but involves the recognition that finance can be scientifically understood in a quantitative way and controlled by a science-based technology.

11.2 Defining the business problem

A number of interviewees noted the importance of not losing sight of the business problem. Tod Loofbourrow, president of Foundation Technologies, a Cambridge, Massachusetts consultancy applying machine intelligence to financial applications, remarks that it is fundamental to define the risk/return profile of the application under development. He also remarks that a fundamental step is establishing a measuring system to evaluate performance.

Inderjit Sandhu, senior technology consultant at Barclays Bank, remarks that business advantage is the sole motivation for implementing adaptive methods. A lot of systems, he observes, have been built but were not really worth it from the point of view of business benefit. Mr. Sandhu argues for what he calls "structured experimentation" and advocates the standard evaluation:

- What do we want to achieve?
- How can we measure our progress?
- How much do we need to do at this stage?
- What is the business benefit?
- What are the risks and how can they be controlled?
- How will the system be implemented and used?

"Keep your feet on the ground," he advises.

First, there is the question of the planning horizon of adaptive methodologies. Norman Packard, co-founder of The Prediction Company, estimates that the timing of a financial forecasting project is in the range of three years. This is the time needed to define the methods, make the first implementations, tune, and go live. The company employs 15 researchers and software engineers working at the cutting edge of technology. The time required will be reduced as researchers move up the learning curve, but at the moment, the effort is measured in years.

Second, and related to the above, is the question of the investment. For John Moody, associate professor of computer science at Oregon Graduate School and founder of Nonlinear Prediction Systems, financial firms are going to have to get accustomed to making significant investments in R&D to keep their firms competitive, much as companies in high-tech sectors do. William Finoff, a former senior researcher in neural network technology at Siemens-Nixdorf and now at The Prediction Company, estimates that the investment required to tackle computer-based financial forecasting is in the range of millions of dollars. He considers this level a blocking factor, as only a handful of financial institutions have the requisite willingness and perseverance.

A third factor is the need to integrate machine-learning methodologies into the global financial technology of the company. As remarked by Paul Refenes, senior research fellow at the London Business School, these methods do not exist in isolation but are the next generation of financial analytics. Put in this perspective, the introduction of adaptive methodologies calls for management attention and business planning.

11.3 Building teams

Building financial applications with machine-intelligence methodologies requires a wide set of skills. Researchers need to master many disciplines, ranging from mathematics and statistics to specific knowledge of neural networks, genetic algorithms, or other adaptive methods. In addition, they need to understand the business problem. The solution has been to build multidisciplinary teams.

Building such teams is a challenge. During the 1980s, most large financial firms in the United States hired teams of physicists, mathematicians, and engineers to work with business managers, economists, and traders. A number of factors facilitated the process. First, the sheer size of the operations allowed the firms to hire relatively large teams of researchers. Universities and research laboratories provided talented scientists experienced in the requisite disciplines. Financial firms were able to build a critical mass of highly skilled people. Cultural aspects helped. Some of these scientists were coming from military laboratories that coupled a high level of theoretical prowess with a goal-oriented pragmatic attitude, and the willingness to work under secrecy.

Another aspect was the involvement of management and the perception that the analytical effort was a genuine building block of a firm's success. The highly competitive environment confronting American banks and financial institutions did not leave anyone the comfortable feeling that it would be possible to shun technology.

Competition, management attention, and critical mass allowed American banks and financial firms to create scientific teams comparable to those found in the physical sciences. Charles Finan, formerly a researcher at the Los Alamos National Laboratory and now director of financial modeling at Cray Research, remarks that the environment inside major Wall Street firms is similar to what can be found in a national lab. The fact that many scientists were hired from the large laboratories helped in creating this environment.

Given the above, the development of models or the adoption of new technologies is tackled like an R&D problem in industry would be. Many U.S. firms have senior managers responsible for new technologies and R&D teams working in close cooperation with business managers.

Building teams, both in-house and with external entities, on an *ad hoc* basis depending on the skill set required, is a widely employed strategy. In the U.S., the Financial Services Technology Consortium (FSTC) links national labs (Lawrence Livermore, Los Alamos, Oak Ridge, Sandia, and FermiLab), major banks (including Bank of America, Chase Manhattan Bank, Citibank, and Wells Fargo), university research centers, and suppliers of information technology in a far-reaching research program on adaptive methods of potentially great interest to banking and finance. In other instances, users team up with third-party suppliers.

In Europe, several factors, either singly or together, have worked against the creation of teams of the size found in the U.S. These factors include the smaller size of operations, limited volumes, and a less competitive environment. New technologies are often explored by small groups of researchers working in relative isolation.

Reaching critical mass has been a problem in Europe. As a consequence, government and universities have served as a driving force in promoting technological innovation. Technology clubs or consortia are used to pull together resources and competencies. Paul Refenes, of the London Business School and cofounder of the NeuroForecasting Club, believes that through such associations it is possible to bring together the required expertise in finance and non-linear techniques.

While building multidisciplinary teams is an issue, it is clear that there is the need to prepare economists and financial specialists with a solid mathematical background. A number of universities are taking steps in this direction. Carnegie Mellon has launched a master of science in computational finance. Students go through a 12-month scientific program, learning to integrate sophisticated mathematical techniques with finance theory and computer technology. The large scientific and computational resources of the university, including the Pittsburgh Supercomputer Center, are available to the students.

11.4 In-house or external development

Most big financial firms interviewed for this book employ large staffs for applications development in areas such as expert systems, financial modeling, and trading systems. Information technology (IT) staffs often represent close to 20% of a firm's total employees, and persons involved in modeling can represent some 1/4 to 1/3 of the IT staff itself. An important issue is whether internal development will continue or if an adequate commercial software offering will develop.

Most firms have reasons for continuing in-house development. Jeffery Butler, chief information officer at Countrywide Funding, cites his company's strategic internal development effort. Morgan Stanley's Charles Marshall, vice president for fixed-income research, believes that applications development is such a dynamic, fast-changing, and time-critical process that outside suppliers find it impossible to cope with it. SBC Warburg's head of global equity derivatives research, Gary Gastineau, finds that those who use quantitative models tend to develop their own. It is, he says, a question of confidence: they want to own the codes.

Financial firms have seen software development costs grow steadily over the past few years, driven by the need to build new models and trading applications. To meet this demand, one Wall Street firm reported hiring 800 IT staff in 1993 alone. The need to control costs is, however, growing. More than one firm mentioned this as a priority.

One strategy for reducing costs is to reuse models. Another strategy could be to turn to outside suppliers. There are difficulties here, though. Large financial firms have developed integrated systems, and third-party programs do not integrate easily. However, Rod Beckstroem, founder of the capital markets software firm C*ATS, believes that object-oriented techniques will provide a solution to the problem of integration.

If the experience of scientific programming in other sectors can be a guide, a commercial offering will develop. Some of the pieces are already in place. Optimization and financial engineering are areas where software packages based on machine-intelligence methods are currently available. A broadening market will allow software companies to invest more, adding features to their products, thus increasing demand and producing a positive spiral.

A similar path could be followed in financial analytics and forecasting applications with the adoption of commercial software or services. Olsen & Associates has placed their forecasting service in some fifty financial institutions. BARRA counts hundreds of users of its multifactor models. Financial risk management software from Algorithmics, GAT, and Kamakura is used worldwide. There is a also a commercial offering in highly specialized niche software. A-J Financial Systems supplies interest rate derivative models based on the academic research of the company's founders John Hull and Alan White.

J.P. Morgan has made its risk management software available. This move is perhaps related to another problem, the role of regulators. It is likely that regulatory authorities will want to know more about the way financial risk is computed, exposures hedged, and so on. This requires a rather open attitude from market players regarding their procedures, and ultimately works in favor of standard software.

As is typical in scientific programming, proprietary methods give a competitive edge for awhile, but competitors catch up as technology spreads. At this point, proprietary development might become a burden. Mr. Beckstroem believes that the market for commercial financial software will evolve as the mechanical computer-aided design (CAD) market did: some twenty years ago major players started developing their own software, but now use commercially available CAD packages.

Another factor in software development is what IBM calls "middleware," software packages that serve as the building blocks of larger applications. A number of such packages are already on the market: smart user interfaces, genetic algorithms, software like Quantum Development's Quantum Leap for business modeling and optimization, parallel databases like DB2000, and neural network software environments like Siemens-Nixdorf's SENN.

There are reasons to consider it likely that a commercial software and service offering will shape up. Growing development costs, requirements for data, the ability to profit from a variety of experiences, even the regulators are arguments in its favor. There might, however, be factors that will hold up this development.

Among them are a preference for proprietary development, internal resistance to change when large staff are already in place, and the difficulty commercial suppliers might have in maintaining their growth and requisite investment levels.

11.5 Adaptive methods and the global context

The depth of use of machine-learning methods in finance varies greatly from country to country. Interviewees attributed this difference to a number of factors. First, it is a question of the size of operations and the level of competition. Joseph De Feo at Barclays Bank remarks that the enormous risk flows involved explain the development of mathematical techniques on Wall Street, while the competitive environment in the U.S. banking sector forced financial institutions to adopt more aggressive strategies, making greater use of technology.

Management culture was also cited. As already seen, management support of technology is critical to successful implementations, and thus is an important differentiator. American management in general shows a greater openness to technology. A culture of academic entrepreneurship, typical in the United States and to some extent in the U.K., was also mentioned as a factor, as science and technology are transferred to industry.

Another factor is the role played by major research centers and universities as suppliers of skill sets. In the U.S., the defense industry has provided scientists who have cut their teeth in non-linear computational methods. Pasadena, California-based Countrywide Funding drew on the experience of aerospace engineers from the nearby Jet Propulsion Laboratory and from aircraft manufacturers McDonnell Douglas and Lockheed in designing their expert system. The Financial Services Technology Consortium, a group of five national laboratories and major banks in the U.S., is another example of defense-related know-how being used to tackle problems in banking and finance.

In the U.K., the London Business School and University College London, backed by the Department of Trade and Industry's Neural Computing Technology Transfer Program, created the NeuroForecasting Club, which recently completed its three-year mission. In Switzerland, the Federal Institute of Technology-Zurich, together with the country's three largest banks, has initiated the Risklab for precompetitive research in risk management.

Correct evaluation of the environment is an important management task in planning adaptive methodologies. How and where to find the requisite skills, where to turn for cooperation, and the likely level of competition are all factors that might influence management in deciding about advanced methods.

12. Future Scenarios

We asked interviewees to comment on the impact that advanced computational technologies would have on financial institutions and on the sector as a whole. We would like to thank them and share with you, pell-mell, some of the scenarios. Only the future will tell how well our interviewees performed as forecasting systems.

"Automation will hit finance as it has hit agriculture and industry, replacing people with machines, creating dislocations. The dealing rooms of the future will resemble today's automated automotive factories."

Matt Ridley, author of *The Economist*'s "Survey of the Frontiers of Finance: The Mathematics of Markets"

"Commodities and foreign exchange trading will be the first to adopt automated trading based on adaptive computational methods. The success of these systems in the equities markets will depend on their ability to capture and integrate fundamentals. Though their adoption will be gradual, automated systems will execute a majority of all trades within the next 10, 20 years."

John Moody, associate professor of computer science at the Oregon Graduate Institute

"The future scenario will witness the integration of various technologies: non-linear statistics for preprocessing data, adaptive

143

*techniques for forecasting plus some form of fuzzy logic to handle
uncertainties, classifiers for building automatically rule-based systems and an eventual revival of expert systems. Efforts will be made
to offer explanations, moving adaptive techniques out of the "black
box" model. Adaptive techniques will be adopted with caution,
leaving decision-making to humans, but shifting the tasks of understanding and exploration to the computer models."*

Eduard Ritscher, vice president for corporate emerging technologies, Chase Manhattan Bank

*"We are talking about evolution, not revolution. Year after
year, these technologies will be increasingly adopted as people
get used to them."*

Michel Hoevenaars, manager of the information technology
research department, ING Bank

*"We are talking about a revolution whose impact will be
absolutely massive and far-reaching. Many people in the industry
are not thinking through the implications."*

Andrew Freeman, banking correspondent, *The Economist*

*"There are two possible scenarios: forecasting models pro-
liferate and there is convergence to best models with sudden
jumps as the market reacts to news and then nothing happens for
a long time; alternatively, forecasting models could destabilize
the assumptions on which much of the derivatives pricing is
based, leading to resistance against them."*

Andrew E. Johnson, quantitative analyst, SBC Warburg

*"Trading will become faster, more volatile. Institutions will
try to create better trading systems, inaugurating an innovation
spiral as big players try to implement a second generation of*

neural net-based forecasting systems and small players try to gain or maintain a market advantage."
Thomas Schmitt, journalist, *Handelsblatt*

"These technologies will give an incremental advantage."
Hans-Otto Isbert, head of the Neural Network Competence Center, Siemens-Nixdorf

"Intelligent computers will change the present day evaluation on the forecastability of the markets. We will see an arms race between computers that will constantly undermine their own success."
Matt Ridley, author of *The Economist*'s "Survey of the Frontiers of Finance: The Mathematics of Markets"

"Over the next years, process control — helping management oversee trading, raising warning flags — will represent the most important application area for forecasting. Another major use will be as a tool, often designed by the trader himself. We will see the beginning of the employment of automated trading systems. They will not do as good as traders, but for some firms they will do good enough. Ten years down, there will be a greater diffusion of automated trading systems. If the number of systems is relatively small, then greater instability could result. However, a high degree of personalization in automated systems is likely: every institution trades differently, with different objectives."
Blake LeBaron, associate professor of economics, University of Wisconsin-Madison

"We are going to see Star Wars. There will be different strategies but certainly a massive use of non-linear technology to forecast markets, volatility, portfolio selection. Digital feeds, power-

ful workstations and quants will provide the decor in which sys-tems and forecasting models will trade against each other. The heavily armored will employ massive computing power and use lots of data; others will take a guerilla-like approach."

Joerg Fricke, systems vice president, Bank Sal. Oppenheim Jr.

PART IV
THE MATHEMATICS OF
UNCERTAINTY AND LEARNING

13. THE MATHEMATICAL HANDLING
OF UNCERTAINTY

Chapters 13-16 offer a brief overview of some of the financial mathematics discussed in the previous chapters. Chapter 13 outlines the classical probabilistic handling of uncertainty in finance; Chapter 14 reviews the mathematical representation of security markets; Chapter 15 covers market constraints and the mathematical treatment of efficient markets; and Chapter 16 sketches some of the topics at the frontier of research referred to previously and shows how adaptive methods fit into the classical framework. Chapter 17 covers the adaptive, data-rich computational methods most frequently used in finance. The emphasis is on key concepts. Readers interested in a comprehensive treatment of the subjects are referred to the literature cited at the end of each chapter.

13.1 Uncertainty and probability
Uncertainty in finance is handled through the notion of probability. Probability is not the only way of handling uncertainty. Non-probabilistic handlings of uncertainty also exist and will be briefly discussed. In the neoclassical framework of finance, however, probability is the key concept.

There are three different notions of probability:

• probability as "intensity of belief" (J.M. Keynes, 1921);

- probability as "relative frequency" (R. von Mises, 1928);
- probability as an axiomatic mathematical theory (A. Kolmogorov, 1933).

The axiomatic theory of probability, developed by the mathematician Kolmogorov, gave probability a rigorous logical foundation. It is at the heart of mathematical finance and is behind the purely axiomatic development of the theory of financial markets.

There are several interpretations of probability in finance; each presents its own conceptual difficulties. There being only one economy, it is not possible to use an "ensemble" view of probability, where probabilities are approximated by relative frequencies, as is customary in the physical sciences. Rather, one takes an axiomatic view of probability and derives consequences regarding time statistics.

Probability in finance is also used to represent individual judgment. We will come back to this later. Let's first summarize the key concepts of probability theory as it is used in finance. Mathematical difficulties are related to continuous-time finance, a hallmark of modern finance theory. We will explore separately the finite case, which is more intuitive than the infinite one.

13.2 Outcomes and events
The intuitive notion of probability is related to observing some phenomena characterized by a range of values about which we are uncertain. This approach immediately leads to the notion of a random variable whose value is governed by probability. Although quite intuitive, this approach might make it difficult to understand how different variables are related.

To understand probabilistic relationships between different observations, it's necessary to reach a higher level of abstraction and to consider the primary objects on which probabilities are defined. In fact, the exposition of mathematical finance starts with the consideration of uncertainty related to states of the economy. These states form the primary structure of probability. An understanding of how probabilities can be assigned to abstract objects is necessary to an understanding of finance theory. The following paragraphs outline how probability theory is logically constructed.

Probability theory starts by considering all possible *outcomes* of an experiment. The set of all possible outcomes is the space Ω on which probabilities are built. *Events* are subsets of Ω that respect a number of restrictions. Probabilities are defined on the events. If we throw a pair of dice, an outcome is a specific pair of possible faces, for instance 3+5; an event is a set of outcomes, for instance all outcomes whose sums are even. Outcomes and events are idealizations distinct from the actual result of a physical experiment.

A simple experiment such as throwing a pair of dice is characterized by a single number. It is important to understand, however, that one can perform many different observations or "measurements" on experiments. In general, experiments are not completely characterized by a single quantity. For instance, a state of the economy is characterized by a large number of possible observations about prices, rates, and other quantities. Probabilities are assigned to sets of states of the economy; probabilities of prices, rates, and other quantities are derived from these more basic objects.

To define probabilities, some structure is imposed on the class of events. The class of events, which we will call $\mathfrak{F}$, has the following properties:

1) the class of events $\mathfrak{F}$ is not empty, i.e., it has at least one member;
2) if an event A belongs to $\mathfrak{F}$, then its complement A' also belongs to $\mathfrak{F}$;

3) if each event *Ai* belongs to $\mathfrak{F}$ for *i=1,2,...*, then their union
    UAi belongs to $\mathfrak{F}$.

Any class with the above properties is called a σ-algebra. A class is called an algebra if property (3) is valid only for a finite number of sets. These concepts might seem a bit abstract, but they correspond to simple, intuitive properties. Condition (1) is a mathematical condition to avoid statements about empty classes, statements that would lead to logical fallacies. Condition (2) ensures that we can consider the set of outcomes that have a given property as well as the set of those that do not have that property. Condition (3) ensures that we can group together different properties and consider a composite property.

In finance theory, we need to work with many different algebras or σ-algebras defined over the same set of states Ω. As we will see in detail later, these structures represent the propagation of information and the consequent reduction of uncertainty.

One space of particular importance in the theory of probability is the *n*-dimensional Euclidean space, i.e., the set R^n of all *n*-uples of real numbers. The smallest σ-algebra that contains the set of all generalized rectangles open on the left plus their unions and intersections is called $\mathfrak{R}^n$. The $\mathfrak{R}^n$ are fundamental for defining random variables, as they characterize a class of subsets of real numbers on which it is reasonable to define a probability structure. The set of all subsets of Euclidean spaces would be too rich; the smaller classes would not be rich enough. The $\mathfrak{R}^n$ are a sufficiently rich set.

13.3 Probability
Probabilities are numbers between zero and one assigned to each event in such a way that the sum of probabilities of disjoint events is the probability of the union of events. From the point of

view of mathematical theory, probability is a set function that respects a number of properties. How probabilities are assigned is not handled by the axiomatic theory.

Formally, probability is defined by a triple $(\Omega, \mathfrak{F}, P)$, called probability space, where Ω is the set of possible outcomes of an experiment, $\mathfrak{F}$ is a σ-algebra of events, and P is a probability measure defined as follows.

A probability measure P is a real function defined over $\mathfrak{F}$ that satisfies three conditions:

1) The probability $P(A)$ is a number between 0 and 1 for any event A that belongs to $\mathfrak{F}$;
2) The probability of the empty set $P(O)$ is equal to 0 and the probability of the entire space $P(\Omega)$ is equal to 1;
3) The probability $P(UAi)$ of any finite or denumerable sequence of disjoint events is equal to the sum of their probabilities $\Sigma P(Ai)$.

Note that, contrary to what might seem intuitive, probabilities are assigned to events, not to outcomes. In the discrete case, however, if there are only a finite number of outcomes, probabilities are assigned to individual outcomes and the probability of an event is simply the sum of the probabilities of its outcomes. Discrete probability models provide a highly intuitive model for understanding probability in finance.

Because continuous models are now a major tool of financial modeling, it's important to understand probability settings in the continuous case. In this case, any single outcome has a probability of zero; it is not possible to calculate the probability of a set by adding up the probabilities of its members. In fact, any finite numbers assigned to individual outcomes would produce infinite sums in the continuous case; probabilities are assigned to events, i.e., sets of outcomes.

Two events are called independent if the probability of their intersection $P(A \cap B)$ is equal to the product of their probabilities $P(A)P(B)$. This definition generalizes in obvious ways to n events. The conditional probability of event A given event B, written as $P(A/B)$, is the probability: $P(A/B)=P(A \cap B)/P(B)$.

13.4 Measures and integrals in finance theory

A number of probabilistic concepts used in financial modeling should now be introduced. These are the notions of measure and of integrals, the notion of random variables, the treatment of the evolution of probabilities with time (stochastic processes), and the notion of the propagation of information. These concepts form the basis of the modern treatment of mathematical finance.

The notion of measure is an extension of the concept of probability. A measure is a set function, denumerably additive, defined on the sets of an algebra (but not necessarily a σ-algebra) that takes value *0* over the empty set but can take any positive value, including, conventionally, an infinite value. A probability is thus a measure of total mass *1*.

Formally, a measure written as M is a function from $\mathfrak{F}$ to R (the set of real numbers) that satisfies three properties:

1) The measure $M(A)$ is a positive number for any set A that belongs to $\mathfrak{F}$;
2) The measure of the empty set $M(O)$ is equal to *0*;
3) If Ai is a finite or denumerable sequence of disjoint sets that belong to $\mathfrak{F}$ and if their union UAi also belongs to $\mathfrak{F}$ then $M(UAi)=\Sigma M(Ai)$.

The notion of measure allows definition of a concept of integral that is fundamental for probability and generalizes the familiar notion of the Riemann integral. The integral is a functional, i.e., it is a number that is associated to every integrable function. It is defined in two steps. Assume, first, that the function f is non-negative and consider a finite decomposition of the space Ω, i.e., a finite set of subsets Ai whose union is the set Ω. Then consider the sum: $\Sigma \, inf(f(w): w \in Ai)M(Ai)$.

The integral $\int f dM$ is defined as the superior, if it exists, of these sums over all possible decompositions of Ω.

Given a generic function f not necessarily non-negative, consider its decomposition into its negative and positive parts. The integral of f is defined as the difference, should a difference exist, between the integrals of the positive and the negative parts. The integral can be defined not only on the entire space, but also on any subset that belongs to $\mathfrak{F}$. It is appropriate to note that the integral is always defined with respect to a measure.

The integral as defined above is meaningful for abstract measure spaces. It allows one to perform the operation of integration directly on the space on which probabilities are defined. It also generalizes the notion of integration related to spaces formed by real numbers. A number of integrals of interest in probability are defined over the real line R and over the Euclidean n-dimensional spaces R^n (the set of real numbers and the set of n-uples of real numbers, respectively).

13.5 Random variables

Probability as a measure over an abstract space of events was defined above. To make probabilistic computations and to represent quantitative observations, however, it is desirable to work with numbers. The notion of random variables transfers probabilities from the original space Ω into various spaces made up of real numbers. Random variables are the conceptual tool for representing quantitative observations or "measurements." In finance, an observation could be the price at which a security was traded or a bid-ask quote.

A random variable X is a function $X(\omega)$ defined over the space Ω that takes values in the set of real numbers subject to the restriction that the set $(\omega: X(\omega) \leq x)$ belongs to the σ-algebra $\mathfrak{F}$ for every real number x. In other words, all outcomes whose corresponding value X is less than x form an event. If a security price is represented as a random variable, the condition that prices are less than or equal to a given amount identifies an event in the basic set of states.

The above condition implies that the inverse image of an interval is an event. It is easy to show that the inverse image of every union and intersection of intervals is an event as well. In general, the inverse image of any set that belongs to $\mathfrak{R}^1$ is an event. This property is also expressed by saying that the function $X(\omega)$ is *measurable* $\mathfrak{F}/\mathfrak{R}^1$. A random variable is, therefore, a measurable real function.

The notion of *measurable function* has an intuitive meaning that is important in finance theory. If a function is measurable $\mathfrak{F}/\mathfrak{R}^1$, this means that the variable X cannot identify any structure finer than $\mathfrak{F}$. Any single value of a random variable identifies an event; a random variable thus has constant value over some event. Knowledge of the random variable's value does not allow discrimination between outcomes within those events. In the finite case, the set of values of a random variable identifies a partition of Ω. This partition is contained in $\mathfrak{F}$.

As already remarked, a random variable represents one possible *measurement* performed on a system. It does not, in general, capture the entire uncertainty structure. A random variable could, for instance, represent a security price at a given moment; the economy's structure of states is much richer.

Given a random variable X, the expected value of X, $E[X]$, is its integral with respect to the measure P: $E[X]=\int X dP$, where the integration is extended to the entire space Ω. In the finite case, the expected value of a random variable is the sum of its possible values, each weighted with its corresponding probability: $E[X]=x_1 p_1+...+x_N p_N$.

13.6 Distributions and distribution functions

Probabilities are set functions defined on abstract spaces. One would, in practice, like to use the many tools of mathematical analysis to compute probabilities. Distribution functions are key concepts to this end.

Consider a random variable X and a set of real numbers A that belongs to $\mathfrak{R}^1$. The inverse image with respect to X of A, $X^{-1}(A)$, belongs to $\mathfrak{F}$, and thus has a well-defined probability $P(X \in A)$. The probability P therefore induces another probability on the real line. This latter is called the distribution or the distribution law of the random variable X and is given by: $p(A)=P(X \in A)$. It is easy to see that this measure is a probability measure. A random variable transfers on the real line the probability originally defined on the space Ω.

The function F defined by: $F(x)=p(-\infty,x]=P(X\leq x)$ is called the distribution function of the random variable X. If a function f such that $P(A)=\int_A f dx$ exists for every set A that belongs to $\mathfrak{R}^1$, the function f is called a probability density and the probability P is said to have probability density f.

13.7 Random vectors

The next step is to consider probabilities related not to a single random variable but to a set of random variables. It is possible to consider random vectors, i.e., finite sets of random variables, denumerable sequences of random variables and, lastly, sets that associate a random variable to a generic index. An example of the latter are stochastic processes that associate a random variable to each instant of time t, where the time index can be discrete or continuous.

Consider a random vector formed by n variables. The key conceptual step is to define joint probabilities, i.e., the probability that the n variables all be in a certain set. A single random variable transfers probabilities from the original probability space to the real line. If a set of n random variables are considered together, it is natural to transfer probabilities from the original probability space to the n-dimensional Euclidean space, i.e., the space of n-uples of real numbers.

On the real line, we considered $\Re^1$ as the natural σ-algebra of events. The σ-algebra $\Re^n$ is the natural choice in n dimensions. As we remarked above, $\Re^n$ is a sufficiently rich set on which standard tools of analysis are meaningful. It is obviously necessary to show that a set of n random variables project the original probability space into $\Re^n$. It can be demonstrated that a random vector formed by n random variables X_i, $i=1,..,n$, induces a probability distribution over $\Re^n$.

13.8 Time and information in finance theory

Following notions introduced by Kenneth Arrow and Gerard Debreu in the 1950s, uncertainty is represented by the space Ω of all possible states of the economy in the period under consideration. Every state is a possible complete history of the economy over a finite or infinite period. At the beginning of the period, the state that will actually be realized is not known.

Kenneth Arrow extended the notions of microeconomics — and thus the analysis of competitive markets — to a set of states that are uncertain. The key idea is that, at any moment, agents trade contingent commodities, i.e., commodities that depend on a particular state of nature to be realized. Standard microeconomic theory, and in particular the analysis of consumer preferences, can be extended to this setting in a natural way. If a probability structure is then imposed on the states, it is possible to extend the above analysis to a probabilistic setting.

Consider the space Ω of all the possible states of the economy, a σ-algebra $\mathfrak{F}$ of events and its sub σ-algebras, and a probability $P(A)$ defined over the events. Each element in Ω is a complete history of the economy over a certain period. If a discrete number n of intervals is considered, every state represents the evolution of the idealized economy over n finite intervals. If an infinite number of intervals or continuous time is considered, the evolution must take into consideration infinite instants.

Information in finance is represented through the concept of an *information structure* or *filtration*. This is a rather difficult, abstract concept. Its intuitive meaning is the following. At the beginning of the period, there is complete uncertainty regarding the state of the economy. The economy is in one particular state but there is uncertainty as to what state will be realized. As time passes, information is revealed by progressively constraining the set of events to which the actual state belongs. Uncertainty is reduced by ruling out possible sets of states. At the end of the period, the actual state is revealed. The conceptual difficulty of the notion of filtration consists in abstracting from news to growing constraints on admissible events.

Formally, the concept of information structure or filtration consists in characterizing all events that become known at a given moment. It is assumed that it is possible to associate to each instant a sub σ-algebra $\mathfrak{F}_t$ included in $\mathfrak{F}$ formed by all events that are known at time t. It is assumed that events are never "forgotten," i.e., $\mathfrak{F}_t$ is part of $\mathfrak{F}_s$ if $t<s$. A filtration, written as F, is this growing sequence of the σ-algebras $\mathfrak{F}_t$ associated with instants t.

This concept might seem counter-intuitive. In practice, at any moment, we form an opinion on the uncertain evolution of the future course of the economy in function of information from various sources. Information (news) seems to bring genuine knowledge and to produce evaluations through learning and reasoning. In finance theory, however, the probability structure of the economy is fixed at the start. The passing of time reveals which of a set of well-defined paths the economy is taking; news reports what is in effect happening.

It is assumed that every random variable is measurable with respect to a sub σ-algebra $\mathfrak{F}_t$; every random variable is therefore associated with a specific time. A time-dependent random variable, i.e., a set of random variables each associated with a specific instant, is called a *stochastic process*. As each stochastic variable is measurable with respect to a sub σ-algebra $\mathfrak{F}_t$, the related process is called an *adapted stochastic process*, or a process *adapted* to the filtration F. The fact that a process is adapted to a filtration means that — at every instant — it is impossible to distinguish between states that will be revealed in future instants.

In discrete models with only a finite number of states and time intervals, it is convenient to represent information structures through the notion of *partitions*. A partition of the space Ω is a class of disjoint subsets of Ω whose union is the set Ω itself. A partition A is said to be finer than a partition B if any set of A can be formed by a disjoint union of sets of B. A partition generates an algebra as the smallest algebra containing that partition. Conversely, any algebra can be generated by a partition. A filtration is thus implemented by an increasing sequence of partitions. Partitions become finer over time, as more information is revealed.

The representation of an information structure through an increasing sequence of partitions lends itself to a representation of the economy as a tree. Consider a finite economy that can assume a finite number of states. Information is revealed in a finite number $T+1$ of instants where trading takes place. The economy starts at time 0 with complete uncertainty regarding the state that will be realized. At each of the $T+1$ instants, a partition is revealed. By this we mean that it becomes known to which event the realized state belongs. At successive instants, partitions are refined, restricting the state to events that are subsets of the previous ones, thereby creating a tree structure. Figure 1 depicts a three-period, six-state economy in a tree format. At time 0, all six states are uncertain; at time 1, it becomes known to which of the three possible events the realized state belongs; at time 2, it becomes known which of the six states is realized.

A filtration or information structure is implemented by a growing sequence of σ-algebras of states. In general, however, we do not know the fundamental structure of states but can only perform *measurements* as, for instance, revealing prices at each trad-

Figure 1
Tree representation of an information structure

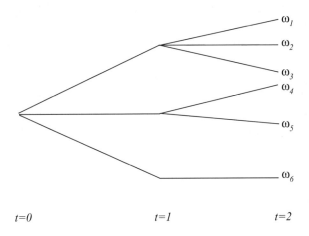

$t=0$ $t=1$ $t=2$

ing date. To see the relationship between a filtration and successive measurements, let's consider the finite case, where filtrations are generated by partitions.

In the finite case, each measurement identifies an event that belongs to a partition. Suppose, for simplicity, that we are restricted to an economy that consists of only one stock whose prices are known at the $T+1$ trading dates. Each state of the economy is a sequence of $T+1$ prices, i.e., a complete history of the economy. The price revealed at any trading date identifies an event. This event includes all price histories with that specific price at that specific date. At the first trading date, the first event is revealed: it is the event formed by all states that have that specific price at the first trading date. As more prices are revealed, events are further constrained and thus belong to finer partitions. They are formed by all states that show the prices revealed thus far. In general, there will be many securities, each described by a price process and a dividend process. States will be the possible paths of these quantities.

In the continuous case, the question is more delicate, as there is no simple and convenient way to associate filtrations and partitions.

A filtration reveals information that is certain. In fact, each state can be seen as a deterministic path in the economy. There is uncertainty only as to what state will be realized. This uncertainty is modeled through a probability structure. There is no uncertainty, however, as to the set of possible states. If the evolution of the economy is depicted as the time evolution of security prices and dividends, each state will be a possible price and dividend path. As we will see, the notion of arbitrage depends only on the states and does not involve probabilities.

The notion of filtration marks the distinction between certainty and uncertainty. Some economic concepts depend on certainty, others on probabilistic uncertainty. There is a continuum between the two. One might imagine expanding the set of states, thus enriching the probability structure and relaxing certain assumptions. Conversely, one might reduce the number of states, for instance ruling out very unlikely events. This is more than an academic exercise; it is a basic component of scenario generation for risk management.

13.9 Conditional probability and expectation

Agents are continuously changing their evaluation of probability on the future course of the economy. In the discrete schematization of filtration, changes in evaluation are due to the realization of a specific event in a finite partition. When events are revealed, uncertainty is represented by probability conditional to the revealed event. Agents know the complete probability structure of the economy and adopt — at every instant — the probabilities conditional to the realized event. Conditional probabilities lead to conditional expectations. In the continuous case, the situation is more delicate and one has to introduce, upfront, the concept of conditional expectations.

Intuitively, we can think of the conditional expectation of a random variable as its expected value restricted to some event. A conditional expectation is a random variable that takes, on every event in $\mathfrak{F}_t$, the same expected value as X but is measurable with respect to $\mathfrak{F}_t$. This concept is relatively easy to grasp in the discrete case where the conditional expectation is a random variable that assumes a constant value on the sets of a finite partition that generates $\mathfrak{F}_t$. Its value for each element of Ω is defined by the classical concept of conditional probability. In the continuous case, however, the concept of conditional expectation is more subtle. The random variable that embodies conditional expectations might be constant only over sets of

measure zero, making it impossible to use the standard definition of conditional probability.

Formally, the concept of conditional expectation is defined as
follows. Given a probability space $(\Omega,\mathfrak{F},P)$ and a sub σ-algebra
$\mathfrak{F}_t$, the conditional expectation of a random variable X with respect
to $\mathfrak{F}_t$, written as $E[X/\mathfrak{F}_t]$ or $E_t[X]$ for brevity, is any random variable measurable with respect to $\mathfrak{F}_t$ such that $\int_G E[X/\mathfrak{F}_t]dP=\int_G$
XdP for any set G that belongs to $\mathfrak{F}_t$. It is possible to show that
such variables exist and are unique, except possibly for a set of
measure zero.

13.10 The interpretation of probability in finance
The above paragraphs outlined the axiomatic theory of
probability. Its application is a question of the interpretation
of probabilistic concepts. As noted, there are two major interpretations of probability in finance: 1) as a descriptive concept
for the economy, and 2) as an element of agents' decision-
making processes.

In the physical sciences, probability is used to mean relative frequency. It enters the theory as an axiomatic mathematical theory and is then interpreted by *bridging principles*,
which basically state that probability will be approximated by
the relative frequency of events. There are, however, many subtleties in this concept, which works well in practice because of
the large numbers of similar events under consideration. More
than a theory of uncertainty, probability is, in this sense, an
"ensemble" theory of phenomena. We do not know what happens to individual phenomena, but we know what happens to
sets of phenomena.

The interpretation of probability in finance is, however, different. In finance, probability represents the uncertain development of a single large-scale object. The physical analogy could be

the stochastic representation of weather. In these cases, the obvious conceptual trick is to translate probabilities into time frequencies and time statistics, and to make observations over a sufficiently long period of time. There are a number of conceptual difficulties in the mathematics involved, due essentially to the fact that economic systems change over time. No law yet explains economic evolution over long periods of time. Most economic and financial laws are relatively simple and approximated. They involve parameters that have to be adjusted and can therefore be considered only as local approximations.

In practice, experimental tests assume that systems are stationary, at least during the period in which observations are made. If a probabilistic framework is used, it must correspond to some empirical test that can be performed only through observations repeated in time. If one keeps changing financial parameters in a model that is supposed to work on a much longer time horizon, one should be aware that the numbers might be meaningless.

In finance theory, probability is also used to represent beliefs. It is assumed that agents associate quantitative evaluations of uncertainty to future events and that these evaluations respect the laws of probability. It is possible to make different assumptions regarding the distribution of beliefs. The most stringent hypothesis is that agents share the same beliefs.

Because beliefs are determinant of the decision-making process of agents, and because the collective behavior of agents is responsible for trading and thus pricing, clearly beliefs might enter finance theory. There are a number of questions about probability as the representation of beliefs, in particular "is this a good representation of beliefs?" and "how does the representation compare with reality?" We will come back to this when discussing developments at the frontier of research.

References

Billingsley, P., *Probability and Measure*, Wiley & Sons, New York, NY, 1986.

Cox, D.R., and H.D. Miller, *The Theory of Stochastic Processes*, Chapman & Hall, London, 1994.

Karatzas, I., and S.E. Shreve, *Brownian Motion and Stochastic Calculus*, Springer, New York, NY, 1991.

14. THE REPRESENTATION OF SECURITY MARKETS

The neoclassical theory of finance is a mathematical theory that describes the evolution of financial quantities in a way similar to that of the physical sciences. This implies that the result of actual or possible "measurements" can be predicted through a sequence of logical operations from initial data. A "measurement" could be the observation of market prices, but it could also be a conceptually more complex operation such as the evaluation of volatilities.

It is important to observe that, in finance as in the physical sciences, the fundamental objective of theory is to make predictions. It is also important to note some differences. First of all, finance theory does not describe laws of nature but a complex artifact, the financial markets. Second, but perhaps more fundamentally, classical finance theory is not a global theory that allows one to compute the evolution of markets from initial conditions.

Finance theory consists of two components:

- a set of relationships that constrains the representation of the market, and
- a set of hypotheses on the evolution of fundamental determinants.

Financial models depend on both components. The choice of models must take into account their ability to describe the functioning of markets as well as their ability to capture the

165

evolution of fundamental risk determinants. Let's explore first how the theory handles market constraints and then the modeling of risk determinants.

The theory of finance is, in a sense, stratified. First are the broad principles that express the notion of perfect, competitive markets. These are the first principles. Then there is a hierarchy of models that embody these principles in different descriptions of markets and of the evolution of risk determinants.

14.1 The Efficient Market Hypothesis

There are different ways to express the notion of competitive markets in a situation of equilibrium. A powerful formulation, introduced by Paul Samuelson and Eugene Fama, is the Efficient Market Hypothesis. The Efficient Market Hypothesis (EMH) makes the assumption that securities are always fairly priced. It assumes that markets are made up of competent and fully informed agents that act rationally and without impediment to new fundamental information. Competitive pressure keeps securities fairly priced, as any opportunity to realize excess profit is exploited without delay and thus disappears.

The EMH is a strong hypothesis whose acceptance still forms the basis of most finance theory of practical use. The validation of the EMH is an empirical problem. Its solution, however, is not easy: the EMH is a conceptual framework that can be adapted to a number of situations. Let's first describe the formalization of the EMH — a difficult problem solved only in the last decade — and then explore how it can be adapted or partially relaxed.

14.2 The formalization of the EMH

To arrive at a formal description of the EMH, a mathematical description of financial markets must be created and appropriate constraints applied. The EMH makes reference to complex market dynamics with an interplay of supply and demand that keeps prices aligned. Whether this is indeed the case or not, the complex market dynamics behind the EMH still far exceed present scientific capabilities. The EMH can be formulated only as an idealization that does not describe the actual process of competitive trading with its demand and supply schedules, information exchange, and learning. The first idealization is to make abstractions from the actual trading mechanism.

The key idea is to describe financial markets as perfect, competitive markets under conditions of uncertainty. Three concepts are key: no arbitrage, equilibrium, and agent optimality. The no-arbitrage principle is, in a sense, the most fundamental. It can be stated assuming only an uncertain structure of dividends and prices and does not imply any market structure. The other two principles imply a representation of agents.

Following standard notions, financial markets are characterized as sets of stochastic processes that describe the evolution of dividends and security prices. There is an underlying probability structure of states of the economy; each stochastic process is a time-dependent mapping that associates to each state a value of dividends and prices. Formally, this structure is described as follows:

i) It is assumed that the economy can be in one of the states of a probability space $(\Omega,\mathfrak{F},P)$ as previously outlined. A filtration, represented by the sub σ-algebras $\mathfrak{F}_t$, describes how information is revealed in time. Thus the economy is formally represented by a probability space $(\Omega,\mathfrak{F},P)$ and by a filtration F.

ii) Each security is represented by two (adapted) stochastic processes formed by the two time-dependent random variables Si_t and di_t. These represent the price and the cash flows generated by the security. Si_t and di_t are adapted processes with respect to the filtration F, i.e., they are random variables measurable for each instant with respect to the σ-algebras $\mathfrak{F}_t$. Thus all securities are represented, in vector notation, by two stochastic processes S_t and d_t adapted to the filtration F.

We will henceforth assume this representation of markets as standard and, unless stated otherwise, we tacitly assume the above description.

A trading strategy is a sequence of portfolios, one for every moment. A portfolio is a set of numbers that specify the quantity of securities held. If there are n securities, a trading strategy is an adapted process described by n time-dependent random variables: $\theta_t=(\theta 1_t,..., \theta n_t)$. A trading strategy can be viewed as the sequence of portfolios potentially held by an agent. It is an abstract concept, unrelated to any existing agent.

It is generally assumed that there is no impediment to or cost associated with trading and that security *short selling* is possible. As a consequence, portfolios are n-uples of positive or negative real numbers.

The key restriction on the market is the assumption that there is no arbitrage in the economy. The notion of no arbitrage will be defined more precisely later. Essentially, it means that there is no possibility of making a risk-free profit without an investment.

Before proceeding, it is important to note just what type of theory finance is. Finance theory is essentially the mathematical description of a complex object, the financial markets, subject to external inputs. The market is described as a basic probability space of states of the economy, a filtration, and a set of pairs of adapted stochastic processes. We will see later how agents can be introduced as utility functions and maximizing operators, but let's first see how markets can be characterized as systems of prices and dividends.

The fundamental law — the no-arbitrage condition — acts as a constraint on this mathematical structure of dividend and price adapted processes. The end product of finance theory is a set of mathematical representations of financial markets that respect the no-arbitrage condition. This is the most fundamental level of finance theory. It is also the most useful one presently, as today's financial models are based on it.

External inputs to the economy are implicit in the above probabilistic description. This probability structure embodies all knowledge of the economy. From a practical standpoint, it is all we need to know. But as it includes a complete probabilistic description of the economy, this structure is complex. The theory expands market constraints and establishes relationships between processes. In doing so, it shows how a number of quantities can be computed in function of other quantities, for instance, how a derivative's price depends on the underlying. With additional hypotheses, it determines the minimum information needed to describe the system.

The actual market processes are hidden in this structure. In fact, we can add agents as abstract utility maximizers and develop a parallel theory. That agents are price-takers, however, expresses the fact that the theory dictates how agents are consistent with the economy, not how they can shape the economy. Agent optimality does not describe the actual trading process but is only a convenient way of expressing the evolution of trading positions.

The mathematical challenge of the theory is to translate the above generalized structure into models that might be of practical utility and that might pass the test of empirical observations. In this respect, the introduction of continuous-time models can be considered a major achievement. To better understand the theory, however, discrete models are a useful idealization. They are still the basis of practical algorithms. We will first describe discrete models and then consider the representation of continuous-time finance.

14.3 Discrete models

Discrete models assume that there are only a finite number of states, a finite number of trading moments, and finitely many securities. As there are only a finite number of states, a discrete probability is assigned to each of them. Consider $T+1$ instants from $t=0$ to $t=T$. There are n securities, each defined by two adapted processes: a price process Si_t and a dividend process di_t. At time t, a security pays a dividend di_t and is available for trading at price Si_t. It is sometimes convenient to consider prices *cum dividendi*, i.e., the sum of prices and dividends at a certain moment. Each adapted process assumes only a finite number of values. In vector form, we can simply write S_t and d_t to represent the set of processes. A discrete model is thus formed by a finite probability space $(\Omega, \mathfrak{F}, P)$, a filtration F made of $T+1$ algebras $\mathfrak{F}_t$, and discrete processes S_t and d_t adapted to the filtration F.

In a discrete model, random variables can assume only a finite number of values. We can always represent a discrete random variable as a function that assumes constant values over the sets of a partition of the states. The evolution of the adapted processes of a discrete model can thus be represented as a path that passes through one of a finite number of points at a finite number of instants. For example, there are only a finite number of prices a security might assume. A path associates one of a possible finite number of prices to each instant. The time evolution of financial quantities can therefore be represented as a tree.

In the discrete case, a trading strategy θ_t is formed by n adapted processes θi, $i=1,n$, which represent the quantity of each security held at every moment. Each trading strategy assumes only a finite number of values, but there are infinitely many possible trading strategies. It is possible to define the value of a trading strategy as: $S_t^\theta = \Sigma Si_t \theta i_t = S_t \theta_t$ (the last quantity is a scalar product). It is also possible to define the dividend process generated by a trading strategy as: $d_t^\theta = \theta_{t-1}(S_t + d_t) - \theta_t S_t$.

Each state is a representation of the entire evolution of the economy over a given period of time. The concept of filtration describes how information is revealed through time in the sense that uncertainty regarding the events to which that state belongs is progressively reduced. It is possible to take a different approach and consider a finite set of instantaneous states for each moment. In this case, it is necessary to assign transition probabilities, i.e., to define probability distributions at each step in function of the previous step.

A particularly interesting class of instantaneous-state models are Markov processes where the probability distributions at time $t+1$ are a function only of probability distributions at time t. A time-stationary Markov process is completely specified by the matrix of transition probabilities defined as follows: $Pij=P(X_{t+1}=i/X_t=j)$. A particular type of Markov representation is obtained by assuming that, at every step, processes might have only a finite number of increments with specified probabilities. Binomial trees, for instance, assume that processes might change by one of two fixed amounts with two specified transition probabilities.

The two approaches might, at first sight, seem radically different. One feels that there is uncertainty at each step in the evolution of the economy. An approach that considers instantaneous states and transition probabilities might seem more intuitive, more realistic than an approach that assumes that the economy follows a certain determined path throughout the entire period. The latter appears to raise questions of economic determinism.

Determinism, in its present scientific sense, means roughly

that phenomena can be described by mathematical models that allow one to predict the future with sufficient accuracy in function of information available at a given time. In the above financial context, a weaker assumption than determinism is made. It is assumed that the economy can follow only a number of well-defined paths but, as there is uncertainty, we do not know the path that the economy is actually following. In other words, we can describe the set of possible paths but we cannot deterministically identify the path that will be realized. Any *certain* information would be incompatible with the model, as it would lead to arbitrage possibilities. If, on the other hand, instantaneous states are assumed, the economy is still constrained to follow only one of the possible sequences of instantaneous states. The deterministic aspects of the two approaches are equivalent: they can be reduced to the statement that the economy can follow only one of a set of possible paths.

From the point of view of probability, consider the approach of assuming a set of states for each moment and a set of transition probabilities. To define the time evolution of the economy, one has to create joint probability distributions building product spaces formed by sequences of instantaneous states. In this way, a space of states is reconstructed. Each state is a complete history of the economy. A filtration can also be reconstructed.

There are thus two possible approaches. In one, transition probabilities generate both the probability distribution over entire paths and the relative information structure. In the other, the entire set of possible paths can be described upfront, but the revealing of the actual realized path is subject to informational constraints represented by a filtration.

The above considerations underlie modeling issues. Most discrete pricing models are built using the transition probability approach. In risk management models, however, one is often concerned with creating entire scenarios. Scenarios are generated with a deterministic approach and a probability structure is imposed on the entire set of scenarios. The key question here is how to reduce the number of scenarios that are considered realizable.

14.4 Completeness and independence

The above description of security markets did not make any assumptions on eventual relationships between security processes. In general, it is possible to establish relationships between securities, thus reducing the number of independent securities. There are several interesting situations to note. First, a number of securities might depend on other securities *by design*. This is the case with derivative securities, where the actual contract imposes relationship between the dividends of different securities. Second, one might make the *hypothesis* that dividends of different securities are functionally related due to economic reasons. In the one-period economy, for instance, the APT models make the hypothesis that dividends are linearly dependent on a number of basic risk factors. Third, in the one-period economy it can be shown that if there are a large number of securities, a linear relationship always holds approximately. We will come back to this.

An important concept in modern finance is market completeness. In the discrete case, a market is said to be complete if any dividend process can be generated by a trading strategy. A security market is complete if, given an arbitrary process x_t, it is possible to find a trading strategy θ_t such that $d_t^\theta = x_t$. In a complete market, any consumption process, i.e., any stream of cash flows, can be generated by investing some amount in a trading strategy.

In the discrete case, it is easy to see how market completeness is related to the number of states and the number of securities. In the simplest case — the one-period economy — market completeness requires that there be at least as many securities as there are states. If dividends are linearly independent, it is easy to see that any dividend can be generated by a portfolio that can be determined solving a simple system of linear equations.

In the multiperiod case, one generally needs a smaller number of securities than of states, as portfolios can be readjusted at every trading date. It can be shown that market completeness requires at least as many securities as the maximum number of events that can be revealed between two trading dates.

14.5 Standard Brownian processes

Continuous-time representations of financial markets are based on the idealizations proposed by MIT's Robert Merton in the early 1970s that trading is a continuous process and that there are an infinite number of states. Continuous-time models are one of the most important advances of modern finance theory. A large fraction of financial modeling depends on them. There are many (infinite) possible mathematical forms for continuous models. The most popular — those that have changed financial modeling — are diffusion processes described by Ito processes. We will restrict our exposition to these.

The representation of security markets in continuous-time parallels the discrete case. The consideration of continuous time and of infinite states, however, makes the mathematics more difficult. The following paragraphs outline only the essentials of the mathematics of continuous-time finance. Some basic concepts must be introduced: first the notion of Brownian processes, then the concept of stochastic integration and stochastic calculus, and, finally, the notion of Ito processes and Ito's lemma. This is the fundamental inventory of concepts for continuous-time finance.

Brownian processes were introduced in finance in 1900 by Louis Bachelier. It is interesting to note that Bachelier studied Brownian processes a few years before Einstein proposed them as

a model for Brownian motion. Brownian motion is the sponta-
neous motion of a small particle suspended in a liquid. This
motion was first discovered by the British botanist Brown, thus
giving the motion its name. The mathematician Norbert Wiener
gave Brownian motion a rigorous mathematical description and
hence these motions are also called Wiener processes.

Brownian processes are a generalization of the concept of a
random walk. Consider a sequence of independent tosses of a coin
and a point that moves one step to the right for every head and one
step to the left for every tail. The position of the point in time is an
example of a simple discrete random walk. Reducing the time interval between two tosses and the size of steps, we obtain in the limit
a continuous process that gives an intuitive idea of a Brownian
process. A Brownian process is formally defined as follows:

Given a probability space $(\Omega,\mathfrak{F},P)$, a Brownian process is a
stochastic process B_t that satisfies the following conditions:

i) The process starts at 0, i.e., $P(B_0=0)=1$.
ii) For every couple of instants t and s, $t>s$, the increment
    $B_s - B_t$ has a normal distribution with 0 *expected value* and
    t–s *variance*.
iii) For every set of instants $t_0,...,t_n$ with $0 < t_0 < t_1 < ... < t_n$, the cor-
    responding random variables B_t are independent.
iv) For every ω that belongs to Ω, the sample path $f(t)=B(\omega,t)$
    is continuous.

The notion of Brownian process extends to Brownian
processes formed by a vector of n processes Bi_t. In general, we
will write B_t to mean a Brownian process formed by n independent Brownian processes $(B1_t,B2_t,...,Bn_t)$ and Bi_t to mean each
of the components. An n-dimensional Brownian process provides
n independent sources of randomness.

Conditions (i) and (ii) together imply that every B_t is normally distributed. In addition, it is easy to show that $E[Bi_t]=0$ and $E[Bi_t^2]=t$. Condition (iv) is not strictly necessary for the definition of Brownian processes. As continuity is a convenient property, if condition (iv) is omitted, it must be shown how to construct continuous-path Brownian processes. For simplicity, path continuity is assumed as a hypothesis. A Brownian process induces a filtration F that is called the standard filtration. It is possible (but not trivial) to show that standard Brownian processes exist in the sense that it is possible to construct them logically. For any given probability space, different Brownian processes exist.

14.6 Stochastic integration

A key notion in continuous-time finance is that of stochastic integration, a process of time integration given an element $\omega \in \Omega$. A stochastic integral is a random variable. It is defined in two steps, first for simple processes, then in general.

Given a standard Brownian process B_t, also written as $B(t)$, consider the interval $[0,T]$. An adapted process θ_t is called *simple* if there exists a partition of the interval $[0,T]$ formed by the instants $0<t_0<t_1<...<t_N=T$ such that $\theta_t=\theta_{tn}$ for t in the interval (t_{n-1},t_n).

Given a simple adapted process, its stochastic integral at any time t, t_n, $<t<t_{n+1}$, is defined as: $\int \theta_t dB_t = \Sigma \theta(t_i)[B(t_{i+1})-B(t_i)] + \theta(t_n)[B(t)-B(t_n)]$. Note that, given a state, all the $B(t)$ assume a well-defined value that depends on the state. The integral thus defined is a time-dependent random variable.

In general, however, processes are not *simple* and the definition of stochastic integral involves a process of taking limits. One can consider smaller and smaller time intervals and replace the sum with an integral. Given the smoothness conditions on the $B(t)$, this is a reasonable process. We can thus define the stochastic integral $\int \theta_t dB_t$ as a limit of a sequence of random variables. From a rigorous mathematical point of view, one should show that these limits exist and that they define a random variable. As the stochastic integral is a time-dependent random variable defined for every instant, it is a stochastic process itself.

14.7 Trading strategies and trading gains

Brownian processes are important because they provide the fundamental source of uncertainty in a mathematically tractable way. It was long believed that security prices themselves follow Brownian processes. This approach is too simplistic; it cannot capture trends in security price processes. To define the notion of a trading strategy, suppose for a moment that this is indeed the case, i.e., that security price processes are Brownian processes.

Suppose that there are n securities whose prices, *cum dividendi*, i.e., the sum of the market price plus dividends, are given by n standard Brownian processes Bi_t, $i=1,n$, or B_t in vector notation. A trading strategy is an adapted process $\theta_t=(\theta 1_t,..., \theta n_t)$ where θi_t represents the quantity of security i held at time t. The cumulative gain induced by a trading strategy can be defined only through a stochastic integral. Consider first the value $B(\theta,t)$ of a portfolio defined by the strategy θt at time t. It is possible to write: $B(\theta,t)=\Sigma Bi_t \theta i_t = B_t \theta_t$, where the last term is, by definition, the scalar product of the vectors B and θ.

If strategy θ remains constant between the instants t and s, $t<s$, it is possible to define the gain in the interval $[t,s]$ as the difference $(B_s-B_t)\theta_t$. Suppose it is possible to divide an interval of interest $[0,T]$ into n subintervals defined by the instants $0<t_0<t_1<...<t_n=T$. If strategy θ is constant in each of the subintervals, the gain generated by strategy θ with respect to the price process B_t is defined as: $\Sigma \theta(t_{i-1})[B(t_i)-B(t_{i-1})]$.

In general, however, strategy θ varies with time in a continuous way and the previous partitioning is not feasible. It is then necessary to use a process of integration. The gain generated by strategy θ with respect to the price process B_t is defined by the stochastic integral: $\int \theta_\tau \, dB_t$.

One might be tempted to ask if this integral is *really* the gain of the trading strategy. The question is not meaningful. A trading strategy in continuous time is an idealization. Like any scientific idealization, it must respond to only two conditions: logical coherence and empirical verification.

14.8 Ito processes

Standard Brownian processes are a model for the *sources* of uncertainty, not a realistic model for the behavior of securities. A realistic model must be able to capture two aspects: random fluctuations and a deterministic trend. One possible model is provided by Ito processes, a generalization of standard Brownian processes. Named after the mathematician who introduced them, Ito processes are defined by the law:

$$S_t = x + \int \mu_s \, ds + \int \sigma_s \, dB_s.$$

where the first integral is an integral with respect to time, the second integral is a stochastic integral (both integrals extend between 0 and t), μ and σ are two adapted processes, and B is a standard Brownian process.

Ito processes are generally written in their differential form: $dS_t = \mu_t dt + \sigma_t dB_t$. This is a stochastic differential equation that cannot be interpreted as an ordinary differential equation. Its precise meaning is given only by the previous stochastic equation. It has, however, an intuitive representation if one takes a finite approximation: $\Delta S = \mu \Delta t + \sigma \Delta B$. This finite equation shows that an

Ito process is approximated by a discrete process so that, at every interval Δt, the discrete process has an increment that is the sum of two parts, one part proportional to Δt with the proportionality factor μ and a second part proportional to ΔB with the proportionality factor σ.

To run a simulation, it would be necessary to generate three random processes: two of laws μ and σ, respectively, and one with normal distribution to generate the Brownian process B. Taking the finite approximation to an Ito process, one might gain an intuitive understanding of Ito processes by constructing tree representations as in the above discrete case.

Assume then that security prices *cum dividendi* S_t follow an Ito process. Given a trading strategy θ_t, the gain generated by the trading strategy is the stochastic integral $\int\theta_t dS_t$. The integral $\int\theta_t\, dS_t$ is an Ito process defined by:

$$\int\theta_t\, dS_t = \int\theta_s\mu_s ds + \int\theta_s\sigma_s dB_s.$$

14.9 Ito's lemma

A very useful theorem in financial modeling, Ito's lemma shows that if a stochastic process is a function of time and of an Ito process, then it is itself an Ito process whose laws can be determined. This is a very important result; it demonstrates that if a security follows an Ito process, derivative securities likewise follow an Ito process.

The formulation of Ito's lemma is:

Assume that X_t is an Ito process defined by: $dX=\mu dt+\sigma dB$, with μ, σ, and B defined as in the previous paragraphs. Assume, in addition, that $f(x,y)$ is a function of two variables with continuous first and second partial derivatives $f_x, f_y, f_{xx}, f_{yy}, f_{xy}, f_{yx}$. The process $Y_t=f(X_t,t)$ is then an Ito process defined by:

$$dY_t = [\, f_x(X_t, t)\mu + f_t(X_t, t) +$$
$$\tfrac{1}{2}\, f_{tt}(X_t, t)\sigma_t^2\,]\, dt + f_x(X_t, t)\sigma_t dB_t.$$

Ito's lemma can be generalized to processes that depend on several different Ito processes.

14.10 Continuous-time security markets

We are now in a position to define a representation of security markets. A security market with N securities will be represented by N Ito processes that represent the security price processes and by N Ito processes that represent the dividend processes. All these Ito processes are determined by a set of D standard Brownian processes that supply the fundamental source of uncertainty. Each Ito process is determined by two additional processes μ and σ.

There is a probability space and a standard filtration induced by the Brownian processes. All processes are adapted to the standard filtration. The set of Brownian processes are the fundamental source of uncertainty, as they determine how information is revealed by generating the standard filtration.

Any trading strategy is an adapted process. The gain generated by a trading strategy is again an Ito process. Ito's lemma ensures that derivatives can also be represented as Ito processes. As a consequence, it is clear that this security market representation is general enough to accommodate all current securities.

The hypothesis that financial quantities evolve as diffusion processes is a strong empirical hypothesis; it is not compatible with all possible empirical observations. It assumes that price and dividend processes follow empirically verifiable stochastic processes.

Diffusion processes, as remarked, are not the only possible continuous-time processes. Another important category of processes are processes with "jumps" as well as combinations of jump and diffusion processes. More generally, the notion of continuous-time finance could be introduced in the context of a continuous-time abstract filtration that does not assume any specific form for the effective realization of stochastic processes. In fact, most of the results that will be discussed in the following paragraphs remain valid in this broader context. Diffusion and jump-diffusion processes, however, have become a fundamental element of financial modeling. To reduce the level of mathematical abstraction of this overview, discussion has been limited to Ito diffusion processes.

Let's now turn to the exploration of the mathematical consequences of the *first principles* of the economy. We will explore the formulation of the no-arbitrage condition that leads to the price fairness condition of the EMH. We will then see how the no-arbitrage constraint relates to agent optimality and equilibrium.

References

Duffie, D., *Dynamic Asset Pricing Theory*, Princeton University Press, Princeton, NJ, 1992.

Huang, C., and R.H. Litzenberger, *Foundations for Financial Economics*, Prentice-Hall, Englewood Cliffs, NJ, 1988.

Merton, R.C., *Continuous-Time Finance*, Blackwell, Cambridge, MA, 1993.

Milne, F., *Finance Theory and Asset Pricing*, Clarendon Press, Oxford, 1995.

15. THE REPRESENTATION OF MARKET CONSTRAINTS AND ASSET PRICING

15.1 Mathematics and the external world

Let's pause for a moment and review the above. First, we defined a generalized representation of the economy as a probability space over which a number of adapted processes are defined. This representation is deceptively general. It makes two strong assumptions. The first is related to the measurability of random variables and the structure of filtration that prescribes the *known* elements of the economy. The second is that the economy is an *external object* whose probability laws are assumed to be known. In economic terms, this is expressed by saying that agents are price-takers. From a practical standpoint, this would be a rather innocuous assumption were it not for the *self-reflective* properties of the economy. The economy is such that knowledge thereof influences the economy itself.

Knowledge of the information structure and of probability distributions is, in fact, a determinant of the decision-making process of agents. The assumption that there is information known with certainty and that there is a "true" probability distribution imposes a number of consequences. It allows the introduction of the concept of arbitrage, which would be impossible to define without some form of "sure" knowledge of the economy's possible paths. It also forces self-consistency constraints between agents and the economy. These constraints mean that agents must have *rational expectations*, i.e., agents must agree on the structure of states and

183

the mapping of random variables over the states. It has implications, albeit weaker, on the probability beliefs of agents.

It is therefore clear that, given the economy's information structure, assuming an objective probability distribution for the economy has important implications. This assumption poses theoretical constraints on the coupling of an objective probability distribution with information feedback. Attempts are being made to partially relax these constraints without changing the basic schema of the economic representations.

15.2 The no-arbitrage condition

The no-arbitrage condition is a fundamental constraint for asset pricing. It basically says "there's no free lunch"; it is not possible to make money without either investment or risk. The no-arbitrage condition involves only the information structure of prices and events and does not imply any specific notion of agent.

In the discrete case, the formulation of the no-arbitrage condition is simple. We have previously defined the dividend process generated by a trading strategy as: $d_t^\theta = \theta_{t-1}(S_t + d_t) - \theta_t S_t$. Note that the first dividend is the opposite of the initial value of the trading strategy, while the last dividend is the trading strategy's last value. An arbitrage is a dividend process that is never negative and that is strictly positive in at least one state in some instant. An arbitrage is thus a trading strategy that has an initial non-positive cost and generates dividends that are never negative but are positive in some state(s) at some instant.

In the continuous-time case, assume that the price process, *cum dividendi*, of n securities in a market is given by an Ito process: $S_t = (S1_t, ..., Sn_t)$, where each Si_t is an Ito process. Consider now a trading strategy: $\theta t = (\theta 1_t, ..., \theta n_t)$. A trading strategy is called self-financing if: $\theta_t S_t = \theta_0 S_0 + \int \theta_x dS_x$, where integration is extended from 0 to t, $t < T$. The condition of self-financing means that the strategy pays no dividends; any profit is reinvested. It also means that there is no inflow of cash.

The no-arbitrage condition requires that, given any self-financing strategy, the following never occur:

$$\theta_0 S_0 \leq 0 \text{ and } \theta_T S_T > 0 \text{ or } \theta_0 S_0 < 0 \text{ and } \theta_T S_T \geq 0.$$

It should be noted that the satisfaction of the no-arbitrage condition, in the discrete as well as in the continuous case, depends on the specific form of probability distributions only for the determination of the sets of measure zero. In fact, the relationships that define an arbitrage depend on the mapping of random variables to states, not on the probability assigned to events. These relationships are satisfied *almost everywhere*, i.e., for all points except possibly a set of measure zero. As a consequence, the specific form of probability distribution does not affect the no-arbitrage condition and any equivalent probability measure respects the same condition. In a rather loose sense, the no-arbitrage condition is determined only by the elements of the economy that are certain, not by those that are uncertain.

15.3 Martingales

Let's now go on to establish a number of important relationships between the price and dividend processes in a market that admits no arbitrage. We will see how such a market prices a stream of uncertain future cash flows. There are different ways to establish pricing relationships in a market. The following simply assumes that markets can be schematized as in the previous paragraphs, in discrete or continuous time, and that there is no arbitrage opportunity. Pricing relationships can be derived from these conditions. The price fairness condition of the EMH is then placed in this context. First, however, the notion of martingale should be defined.

Martingales have acquired considerable importance in the theory of finance. In informal terms, the concept of a martingale is simple: it is a stochastic process where the conditional expected value of a variable given its present value equals its present value. The notion of martingale translates the notion of "fair game" where the present wealth of a player equals the expected value of his or her future wealth. A fair game, in the discrete case, is exemplified by the cumulative wins and losses by tossing a fair coin. If a player wins a fixed amount of money for each head and loses the same amount for each tail, cumulative wins are a martingale. This means that, at any moment, a player cannot expect to change his or her total accumulated wealth. This is not to say that the player's wealth will not fluctuate, only that the expected value is exactly the present value.

Formally, assuming as usual a probability space and filtration and using the notation of previous paragraphs for conditional expectation, the process $X(t)$ is a *martingale* if the following condition is satisfied:

$$E[X_t/\Im_s]=E_s[X_t]=X_s \text{ for any } t{\geq}s.$$

The condition of being a martingale does not imply that there are no correlations between variables in successive instants but only that the conditional expected value at any future instant is equal to the present value. This is a weaker condition that allows, for instance, the forecasting of volatility.

15.4 Martingales in the theory of efficient markets

Martingales occupy an important place in the description of efficient markets. Remember that in an efficient market all securities are fairly priced. Developing on ideas introduced by Paul

Samuelson in the 1960s, Eugene Fama proposed defining a market as efficient if prices follow martingales.

To understand the reasoning that led to this, it should be recalled that Samuelson introduced the notion of a market where sharp-eyed and well-informed agents rapidly exploit any possibility of making a profit and, in so doing, realign prices. As any forecast is immediately exploited, it seems natural to require that the future expected value of any security be equal to its present values, i.e., that prices follow martingales.

A market model in which stochastic variations are random fluctuations, such as Brownian processes, satisfies the above conditions. It is clear, however, that a standard Brownian process is too simple to describe the evolution of securities. To overcome this problem, Fama defined a market as efficient if *cumulative gains discounted with a constant discount factor follow a martingale.* This idea, put forward in a now famous paper published in 1970, has had significant influence on the theory of finance. It allowed one to take into account a trend of positive returns, retaining a martingale structure. As empirical studies seem to confirm that, in the absence of private information, it is impossible to realize excess profits given the difficulty of making forecasts, the notion that security prices behave as martingales is attractive.

Fama's idea was controversial. It seemed to imply that financial information and analysis is basically futile: engaging in research to reach the conclusion that the pay-off of any strategy is equivalent to that of a buy-and-hold strategy would be wasteful. Within this framework, the notion that only insider trading makes excess profits seems inescapable.

Contemporaneously, the notion of the Capital Asset Pricing Model (CAPM) was being developed. In the CAPM model, an efficient market assigns a price to any claim to future cash flows. The key idea is that, under uncertainty, the market prices future cash flows not only in function of their value but also in function of their risk, i.e., in function of their probability distribution. The market assigns a premium to risk.

The principle of Fama requires that a discount factor for future payments is fixed. This factor cannot be the riskless discount factor, as investors require a premium for bearing risk, and it cannot be constant, as it is determined in function of the riskiness of assets that varies in time. The analysis of Fama could not be accepted in its initial formulation. As it turned out, by creating a special pseudo-probability structure, it is possible to retain the martingale idea and to equate present prices to the discounted expected value of future cash flows. This is the theory of equivalent martingale measures developed in the 1980s by Harrison, Kreps, and Pliska. The notion of prices as martingales thus found its conceptual framework.

The theory of equivalent martingale measures can be developed abstractly, taking into account only the price and dividend processes of securities in a market. It is an asset pricing theory insofar as it determines the present price as an expected value. We will show how the theory is developed in two cases: first in the discrete case, and second assuming that price and dividend processes are Ito processes. This restriction is not necessary, however, and the theory of equivalent martingale measures can be developed for an abstract filtration.

15.5 Price deflators in the discrete case

Consider, first, a one-period setting with only one trading date at time 0 when commodities contingent to states in time 1 are traded. Using the same notation of multiperiod discrete models, consider n securities with prices S and payoffs d where S and d are $n \times s$-matrices that specify the dividend of each security in each state. In this setting, it can be shown that the no-arbitrage condition is equivalent to the existence of a state-price vector π, which is a vector such that: $S=\pi d$. This relationship means that prices are a linear combination of dividends. It also means that prices are a linear combination of state prices, i.e., prices of contingent commodities that pay one unit of dividend in exactly one state and nothing in other states.

This idea can be taken further to the multiperiod discrete model. To show this, the notion of the state-price deflator must be introduced. A *deflator* is a strictly positive adapted process. In the multiperiod discrete model, a deflator is a collection of T positive valued discrete random variables. In this simplified case, a random variable is a real valued function that assigns a real number to each of the n states. Given a price-dividend pair (S,d), a deflator π is a *state-price deflator* if, for all t:

$$S_t=1/\pi_t E_t[\Sigma\ \pi_j d_j]$$ where the sum is extended from $t+1$ to T.

Let's look at the above expression more closely. On the left side there is the vector of security prices S_t. Each security price is an adapted process, i.e., a random variable for each time (adapted to the filtration). For each security, the left side is thus one number for each state. The right side is a vector of adapted processes. The first term is the process reciprocal of π_t obtained by associating to each state the reciprocal of the corresponding π_t. It is easy to show that this is indeed an adapted process. The second term is the conditional expectation of the sum of future dividends d_j, each discounted (multiplied) by the corresponding π_j. This sum is an adapted process and it therefore makes sense to take its conditional expectation at time t, which is, by definition, another adapted process. As a product of two adapted processes, the right side is indeed an adapted process.

If we multiply both sides by π_t, the above expression states that a deflator is a state-price deflator if it provides discount factors so that discounted security prices are the conditional expectation of discounted dividends. This means that at any trading moment there is a finite set of real numbers, one for each state with the following special property. If we multiply the value of the dividends for the corresponding state-price deflator in each state and for each instant, we obtain a new discounted dividend process. The price process discounted by the same factor is the conditional expectation of the sum of the discounted dividends. This property holds for each security.

Consider now the gain process G_t for a price-dividend pair (S,d), which is defined as: $G_t=S_t+\Sigma d_j$, j from 1 to t. Given a deflator γ, the deflated gain process is defined as $G_t^\gamma =S_t\gamma_t+\Sigma d_j\gamma_j$, j from 1 to t. Note that the deflated gain process is not the gain process multiplied by the deflator. It can be demonstrated that π is a state-price deflator if and only if the end-of-period price $S_T=0$ and the state-price deflated gain is a martingale. The condition that end-of-period prices are equal to zero simply reflects the fact that there is no dividend after the end of the period.

The above conditions on prices and gains are equivalent. They say that if we discount prices and dividends with a state-price deflator, discounted prices are the expected value of the future stream of discounted dividends and the cumulative (discounted) gains are a martingale.

We now have to relate the above to the no-arbitrage condition. The existence of a state-price deflator and the no-arbitrage condition means that they are equivalent conditions. In fact, it can be demonstrated that the dividend price pair (S,d) admits no arbitrage if and only if there is a state-price deflator. This shows that, in absence of arbitrage, there are discounting factors so that discounted prices are the expected value of discounted dividends and that it is possible to define a gain process that is a martingale.

15.6 Equivalent martingale measures and complete markets in the discrete case

The next step is to show that the notion of state-price deflators is equivalent to the notion of equivalent martingale measures. In other words, the operation of multiplication for a discount factor is equivalent to modifying probability assignments in some special way.

Suppose first that there is short-term riskless borrowing and define $R_{t,s}$ as the payback at time s of a unit of account borrowed without risk at time t. If $B(t)$ is the price at time t of a riskless bond that pays one unit of account at the end of the period, $B(t)$ is the reciprocal of the payback of a unit of account borrowed without risk at time t and therefore $B(t)=1/R_{t,T}$.

We can now define the concept of equivalent martingale measure. A probability measure Q is said to be equivalent to a probability measure P if both assign probability O to the same events. An equivalent probability measure Q is an equivalent martingale measure if: $S_t = E_t^Q [\Sigma\, d_j\, /R_{t,j}]$ with the sum extended over j from $t+1$ to T and $t<T$. The previous relationship can also be written as $S_t\,/\,B(t) = E_t^Q [\Sigma d_j/B(j)]$. This last expression parallels the corresponding expression of the previous paragraph, substituting $1/B(t)$ for π_t. Under an equivalent martingale measure, security prices normalized by dividing by the price of a riskless bond are the conditional expectation of dividends normalized by the same factors.

In analogy to the previous paragraphs, the above condition can be expressed in terms of deflated gains. In fact, the sum of normalized prices and cumulative normalized dividends, i.e., the sum of prices and cumulative dividends divided by the price of a riskless bond, is a martingale under an equivalent martingale measure.

The previous paragraphs established that the condition of no arbitrage is equivalent to the existence of a state-price deflator π. This result can now be extended. It is possible to demonstrate that there is no arbitrage if and only if there exists an equivalent martingale measure. In addition, it is possible to establish a relationship between a state-price deflator π and the density of the equivalent martingale measure Q with respect to P as follows.

If Q and P are equivalent probability measures, it is possible to show that there is a function f, called the density of Q with respect to P, defined by $Q=\int f dP$. The density f is called the Radon-Nikodym derivative of Q with respect to P and is written as $f=dQ/dP$. The density is a random variable.

In the absence of arbitrage, there is a state-price deflator π and an equivalent martingale measure Q. The two probability measures Q and P are equivalent probability measures and there is therefore a density f of Q with respect to P. It is possible to show that the density of Q with respect to P, i.e., the Radon-Nikodym derivative dQ/dP, is given by: $f=dQ/dP=R_{0,T}\,\pi_T/\pi_0$. In addition, f is a random variable and it is possible to take its conditional expectation. It can be demonstrated that $\pi_t=E_t[f]\pi_0/R_{0,t}$. These relationships work in both directions. Given an equivalent martingale measure, one can construct a state-price deflator and vice versa.

The above results show that state-price deflators and equivalent martingale measures are the same concept. One might take dividends and prices and discount them with a special variable discount factor, the state-price deflator. A state-price deflator is an adapted process. After this operation, discounted prices are the conditional expectation of discounted dividends. Alternatively — and equivalently — one can discount prices and dividends with a riskless rate and modify probabilities. The above used riskless rates as the discount factor. The equivalent martingale measure formulation can be generalized taking as the discount factor the price of any security. Given any discount factor, it is generally possible to find a corresponding equivalent martingale measure.

It is also possible to show that, in the absence of arbitrage, the equivalent martingale measure is unique if and only if markets are complete. If a market is complete, it is possible to price any security new to the market by no-arbitrage arguments using the equivalent martingale measure principle. In fact, completeness implies that any new redundant security can be replicated by a portfolio of existing securities. An option price, for instance, is simply the expected value of its end-of-period price under the equivalent martingale measure.

Fama's notion of efficient markets equates efficiency with the possibility of finding a discount factor so that prices plus cumulative dividends are a martingale. The above proposition gives a precise meaning to this notion. It states that the condition of no arbitrage is equivalent to the possibility of finding a system of discount factors, eventually random and time variable, so that the discounted gain process is a martingale. Alternatively, one might use a fixed system of discount factors, be they the riskless rate or the price process of one of the securities, and modify probability measures.

15.7 Deflators in continuous time

Let's now turn to the continuous-time case. The basic principles are fundamentally the same but the mathematics is more complex and there are technical subtleties to be taken into account. We have first to define the notion of deflator. We assume the market representation discussed in the previous section. There are N securities whose price processes are described by an Ito process $X=(X^1,...,X^N)$ taking values in R^N. Each Ito process, in turn, is determined by D risk determinants represented by D standard Brownian processes. Assume that there is no distribution of dividends so that prices are to be intended *cum dividendi*. Prices and cumulative gains thus coincide. There are a number of technical conditions that must be assumed to ensure that variances and expected values exist when necessary.

As previously defined, the gain of a trading strategy $\theta_t = (\theta 1_t, ..., \theta n_t)$ is the stochastic integral $\int_0^t \theta_t dX_t$.

Assume that there is one security, say X^1, whose price process is deterministic and can be written as: $dX_t^1 = r_t X_t^1 dt$. The rate r is the continuously compounded risk-free rate.

A deflator is a strictly positive process that changes the price scale for every moment by a random factor that depends on time and the state. Formally, given a price process X, a deflator is a strictly positive Ito process Y that produces a new process $X_t^Y = X_t Y_t$.

15.8 Equivalent martingale measures in the continuous case

A state-price deflator π is a deflator so that the deflated price process $X_t^\pi = X_t \pi$ is a martingale. To draw a parallel with the discrete case, assume that there are no dividends. It is possible to show that if a state-price deflator exists, there is no arbitrage.

Recall that a probability measure Q is said to be equivalent to a probability measure P if both measures assume value zero over exactly the same events. Equivalence means that although probability measures might be different for Q and P, the structure of "certain" events (certain in a probabilistic sense) remains the same. A measure Q equivalent to P is called an equivalent martingale measure for the price process X if X is a martingale with respect to Q.

It is possible to show that if a price process admits an equivalent martingale measure, there is no arbitrage. It is then possible to conclude that the no-arbitrage condition is a necessary condition for the existence of both a state-price deflator and of an equivalent martingale measure.

As in the discrete case, it can be shown that state-price deflators and equivalent martingale measures are equivalent concepts. Suppose that Q is an equivalent martingale measure for the process X_t^Y where $Y_t = exp(-\int_0^t r_s ds)$ and consider the density process $\xi_t = E_t(dQ/dP)$. It is then possible to demonstrate that the process $\xi_t Y_t$ is a state-price deflator. In other words, if Q is an equivalent martingale measure, it is possible to have a state-price deflator with two successive deflation steps, first with the process $Y_t = exp(-\int_0^t r_s ds)$, then with the process $\xi_t = E_t[dQ/dP]$.

Conversely, it is possible to show that, given a state-price deflator π, the density process $\xi_t = exp(\int_0^t r_s ds)\pi_t/\pi_0$ provides an equivalent martingale measure. The two propositions express the relationship between state-price deflators and equivalent martingale measures. They mirror the same propositions in the discrete case under the assumption that there are no dividends. It is possible to prove the same results in the case of distributed dividends. This, however, adds mathematical complexity, as there are many different ways to represent dividends in the continuous-time case.

The above demonstrates that the no-arbitrage condition is a necessary condition. In the continuous case, sufficiency is more delicate. Nevertheless, it is possible to show that, under a number of technical conditions, the no-arbitrage condition imposes the existence of an equivalent martingale measure and of a state-price deflator.

In the continuous setting, the question of the equivalence of market completeness and the uniqueness of the equivalent martingale measure becomes more delicate. Positive results can be shown under a number of qualifications.

15.9 Arbitrage pricing and derivatives pricing

We have reviewed the no-arbitrage asset pricing theory for a market where there are a finite number of independent sources of uncertainty represented by a multidimensional Brownian process. For this type of market, under a number of assumptions, two basic results hold:

1) The no-arbitrage condition is equivalent to the existence of an equivalent martingale measure so that discounted price processes are martingales with respect to this measure;
2) If there is no arbitrage, market completeness is equivalent to the uniqueness of the equivalent martingale measure.

In applications, the above propositions are generally assumed. The theory leads to a relative pricing methodology for the pricing of redundant securities. It is based on identifying, in a given market, a set of *primitive* securities so that any other security can be priced by constructing a replicating portfolio. This is the arbitrage pricing theory.

In the previous paragraphs, it was hypothesized that there are D independent risk determinants. In a market model, the number of securities is generally much larger than the number of basic risk factors, the fundamental risk determinants of the system. Once the prices of the basic risk factors are known, any security can be priced by no-arbitrage arguments following the above analysis. Risk factors might be the securities themselves, in which case any *redundant* security might be priced by no-arbitrage arguments constructing replicating portfolios.

The equivalent martingale measure theory forms the basis of most financial modeling techniques today. It shows that after discounting and under the equivalent martingale measure, it is possible to handle valuation problems as if the economy were risk-neutral. In this setting, if there are no dividends, the fundamental result is:

$$S_t = E_t^Q [S_T].$$

The above shows that, at a given time, security prices can always be expressed as the expected values of prices at some future time. This condition is a powerful pricing formula. It is deceptively simple. In fact, it generally translates into a Partial Differential Equation (PDE), of which the Black-Scholes differential equation is an example. If there are dividends, equivalent pricing formulas are available.

15.10 Agent optimality and equilibrium

The theory of efficient markets outlined above is an abstract theory developed for a system of prices and dividends. Agents do not enter into this formulation. We have chosen to expound this part of the theory, as it gives a natural theoretical framework to the idea of the fairness of prices. In addition, the idea that prices can always be determined through an expectation operator is central to present financial modeling and, in particular, to algorithms for derivatives pricing. We will later see how this theory can be related to financial time series forecasting models. Before turning to this subject, we would like to explain the general principles of how, in a classical setting, price behavior is represented through the interaction of agents.

The notion of agents functioning in the market must be translated into some form of mathematical operator. The usual representation describes agents as maximizers of a utility function over a sequence of portfolios. Formally, an agent is represented by the following:

1) a utility function U;

2) an endowment *e* that represents its exogenous financial resources;
3) a trading strategy θ.

It is assumed that agents are price-takers in the sense that their individual actions do not influence the market: an agent might buy or sell any number of securities without influencing the market price. It is also assumed that the trading strategy chosen by each agent maximizes his or her utility function. Utility functions are a convenient way of expressing agents' preferences. A utility function U is a function defined over an agent's consumption process for every state. Lastly, it is assumed that the economy is in a condition of equilibrium. These hypotheses and the no-arbitrage principle are not independent; the theory finds relationships between no arbitrage, agent optimality, and equilibrium.

Based on the notions of agent optimality and market equilibrium, it's possible to develop an asset pricing theory parallel to the martingale pricing methodology. Agents, as mentioned, are defined as abstract utility maximizers. There are many options to choose from in defining the theory of agent optimality and equilibrium. In other words, there are many different models of competitive markets in a situation of equilibrium. In the no-arbitrage condition, different models are characterized by choosing specific hypotheses on the mathematical form of price and dividend processes. If agents are introduced, one has to choose how they are represented.

Before touching briefly on the various possibilities, it is important to remark that all models must respect the condition of no arbitrage. Arbitrage versus no arbitrage is not an available modeling option. In fact, the notion of no arbitrage is substantially equivalent to agent optimality. If a market would admit arbitrage, an optimizing agent would take unbounded positions, realizing arbitrary gains. No market could realistically work under conditions of arbitrage, because it would "explode." Large trades would immediately affect prices and destroy arbitrage conditions.

This is not to say that the no-arbitrage condition is a mandatory condition for any market description. It would be possible to represent financial markets differently from the no-arbitrage equilibrium representation. However, these non-equilibrium market descriptions would imply a different scheme that would allow for some feedback from trading to pricing under conditions of non-equilibrium.

Let's now go back to the question of portraying agents. One conceptual decision is whether agents are assumed to share objective probability distributions or if they are endowed with subjective evaluations. Theories and models that assume objective probability distributions shared by agents essentially formulate *consistency conditions* between agents' decisions and the objective market distributions. Approaches that assume subjective beliefs have, on the other hand, as their starting point, agents with their subjective probability evaluations. This approach might seem more realistic, as live traders do have heterogeneous beliefs. It has to be understood, however, that in its mathematical form, present finance theory cannot handle the learning process of agents. In addition, the theory is unable to handle the feedback effects of individual trades on the market; agents are price-takers.

As a consequence, the notion of heterogeneous beliefs does not fundamentally extend the understanding of how agents can interact with the market. Most results that can be derived can also be derived in the heterogeneous approach. A key tool of both approaches is the representative agent approach: agents are grouped together as a single agent and consistency conditions are determined.

One important point in the understanding of the heterogeneity of beliefs is that agents must agree only on the "certain" elements of the economy. We remarked above that the no-arbitrage condition must be respected. But the no-arbitrage condition depends only on the "certain" elements represented by the set of states, filtration, and by the set of states of zero probability. Agents must share these basic beliefs. In other words, they must agree on the set of states and on the mapping of random variables onto the states.

More radical choices of agent representation might be made by assuming that agents decide, not on the basis of probability evaluations, but on the basis of measures and evaluations of uncertainty different from probability. This is an interesting development. It uses decision-making models that might prove more realistic than those presently used.

Another choice regards the assumptions on utility functions for modeling agents. This is related to the above, as the decision-making model includes both elements of evaluation of uncertainty and preference ordering. Heterogeneous beliefs might, in fact, be assumed simply by diversifying utility functions. There is a vast spectrum of available choices, from expected utility functions to other more general schemes of decision making.

A key question is that of equilibrium. Basically, all of today's theories are dynamic equilibrium theories. The fundamental notion is that markets clear and that there is no unsatisfied demand or excess offer. This would, in fact, imply a price formation mechanism based on actual trading that is presently beyond the possibility of mathematical handling.

Equilibrium theories of market evolution based on the representation of agents are fully developed. Theoretical results in equilibrium asset valuation parallel the arbitrage methodology. There is a remarkable coherence between the two approaches.

From the practical standpoint, the above theoretical developments have impacted asset and portfolio management. The latter apply the principles of agent optimality to construct optimal port-folios. The growth of low-cost high-performance computing power has brought within reach the possibility of large-scale portfolio optimization with important consequences for asset management.

References

Duffie, D., *Dynamic Asset Pricing Theory*, Princeton University Press, Princeton, NJ, 1992.

Fabozzi, F.J., *Valuation of Fixed Income Securities and Derivatives*, Frank J. Fabozzi Associates, New Hope, PA, 1995.

Harrison, J.M., and D. Kreps, "Martingales and Arbitrage in Multiperiod Securities Markets," *Journal of Economic Theory*, 20: 381-408, 1979.

Harrison, J.M., and S. Pliska, "Martingales and Stochastic Integrals in the Theory of Continuous Trading," *Stochastic Processes and Their Applications*, 11: 215-260.

Hull, J.C., *Options, Futures, and Other Derivative Securities*, second edition, Prentice Hall, Englewood Cliffs, NJ, 1993.

Merton, R.C., *Continuous-Time Finance*, Blackwell, Cambridge, MA, 1993.

Milne, F., *Finance Theory and Asset Pricing*, Clarendon Press, Oxford, 1995.

16. At the Frontier of Research

16.1 Research directions

The basic notions behind the mathematical analysis of efficient markets have been outlined. Much research is going on. First, there are efforts to establish better valuation models and hedging strategies in the general context of the no-arbitrage theory. This research is of practical importance, as it leads, potentially, to better valuation models. Second, efforts are under way to extend the basic theory. Third, research is attempting to solve the self-referential problem of finance. Each of these areas of research will be covered briefly.

The quest for better models within the classical framework represents the largest part of today's research efforts. It is motivated by the need to analyze complex securities, to engineer hedging strategies, and to pursue possibilities of trading gains. Most of these efforts are proprietary efforts undertaken by the financial firms themselves. Modelers use whatever mathematical technology might be suitable for modeling securities with complex payoffs and for replicating complex portfolios. Significant progress has been made in the area of optimization techniques. Chapter 17, "Adaptive Computational Methods," describes genetic algorithms, one of these new techniques. Simulated annealing and stochastic programming are also finding their way into financial modeling. It is fair to say that large-scale optimization models are rapidly becoming an effective tool.

One sector attracting growing attention is the modeling of

interest rates for the valuation of fixed-income securities and interest rate derivatives. Following the introduction of arbitrage-free interest rate models, a new generation of interest rate models is being built. In particular, Cornell University's David Heath, Robert Jarrow, and Andrew Morton introduced a new methodology, the HJM model. This has spurred a number of practical efforts to build models using this methodology.

There are efforts under way to capture the forecasting ability of new techniques, leading to better modeling of the basic risk determinants. This chapter will later explore the relationship between the no-arbitrage setting and forecasting.

One important discovery is the volatility clustering effect shown by many financial time series. It has been observed that volatility tends to cluster in periods of high volatility followed by periods of low volatility. This effect is called *heteroskedasticity*. For discrete time series, the ARCH models developed by Robert Engle and their generalization, the GARCH models developed by Tim Bollerslev, describe this heteroskedasticity. Following these works, a family of generalized X-ARCH methods has been developed and is gaining increasing acceptance. Efforts to integrate these findings into the continuous-time framework of financial modeling are being made.

At the frontier of theoretical research is work on the mathematical structure of finance theory. This work consolidates the fundamental mathematical structure of the theory, relaxes various hypotheses, and generalizes results. It is impossible to give even a short resume of the present efforts, but we would like to mention work on the completeness of markets that extends the fundamental results outlined above to the more general context of semimartingale theories and work that considers models with an infinite number of securities.

Attempts to relax some of the hypotheses of efficient markets and to capture non-equilibrium phenomena are related to efforts to improve forecasts. From the practical standpoint, the major effort is in forecasting. These methodologies eschew attempts to formalize a theory of financial markets, concentrating instead on finding interesting properties of financial time series.

Efforts concentrated on improving modeling without departing too much from a classical framework have produced some results. These efforts assume that there are asymmetries in the information process of agents, with some agents better informed than others. Presently, however, the theory is still at the level of the macro aggregation of agents with limited learning abilities. It offers no real framework for non-equilibrium.

The key problem to be solved is the self-referential quality of the economy. Given the level of sophistication of the markets, if one admits that there are objective probability distributions that describe the economy and that these can be scientifically ascertained, agents' beliefs must be in agreement with these evaluations. This is the perspective outlined above: a probability structure is assumed and consistency conditions are derived. Otherwise expressed, agents are price-takers in a competitive market.

Agents, however, do not really *know* future probability distributions the way, for instance, probability distributions are known in quantum mechanics. Agents simply have a level of uncertainty that might be modeled or somehow measured, and make decisions in function of this. The complex interaction of intelligent agents is based on access to information, beliefs, learning, constraints, general principles, and so on.

Rather than assume as a given a probabilistic structure, more realistic models of financial markets should understand how agents work, learn, and trade in the market. They should also be able to make independent forecasts of external events, such as the dividend stream generated by a security. In fact, a realistic forecast must take into account events, agents' perceptions of events, and agents' reactions in a competitive market. Modeling this complexity is exceedingly difficult. Theoretical efforts to build new types of models are under way, but the obstacles are formidable. A number of efforts to build learning models were cited in the previous chapters. One such effort is the artificial market built by W. Brian Arthur and co-researchers at the Santa Fe Institute (NM). These are still highly idealized models of the markets.

16.2 Empirical tests of market efficiency

Ever since the notion of market efficiency was introduced, the problem of its empirical verification has been raised. There is clearly a theoretical interest in this question, as most financial models are based, in one way or another, on market efficiency. There is also a practical interest, as it is widely believed that it is possible to earn excess returns by exploiting market inefficiencies. This supposedly derives from the fact that in an efficient market securities are always fairly priced. The following paragraphs will deal with the conceptual problems of empirical tests of market efficiency. We will also show how the notion of *excess returns* is not well-defined and how the quest for market inefficiencies might be misplaced.

Let's start with a few remarks on empirical verification in science in general. One might be tempted to believe that in the physical sciences empirical verification is, conceptually at least, a simple and straightforward matter of checking the results of experiments. This perspective would be wrong even in the case of physics. The reason is twofold. First, in every empirical test, a mathematical model is compared against a finite number of observations. But any finite number of observations is compatible with an infinity of possible mathematical models. Thus no observation can be conclusive. This is not an academic distinction. There are, in practice, competing frameworks for describing a number of physical phenomena.

In addition, observations are never primary observations but are *theory-laden* in the sense that the results of observations are interpreted through the theory itself. If we change some theoretical hypothesis, the meaning of the observation changes. Cosmology is a case in point: the meaning of a number of critical observations depends on the theory each cosmologist subscribes to.

In finance and economics, one tends to make a distinction between quantities that can be observed, such as prices, and quantities that cannot be observed, such as volatilities. Often the notion of "proxy" — a quantity that can be observed that takes the place of another quantity that cannot be observed — is invoked. It should be noted, however, that in a more mature stage of science this distinction largely disappears. Scientists perform "measurements," i.e., observations that must be interpreted within a theory. Consider the notion of price. If one adheres to a notion of continuous-time finance, prices are represented by time-continuous stochastic processes, which is certainly not what one observes.

The conclusion is that there is always a conventional element in science. We cannot really ascertain if a theory is true or false, but can only build experimental evidence that renders a theory plausible. In addition, scientific theories are global theories: they respond to the empirical verdict only *in toto*. Generally, no single observation is able to produce radical changes. Any theory is typically robust to a number of test failures as theoretical adjustments can be made to accommodate new empirical findings. There are moments, however, where adjustments become too difficult and science goes through a major change in the basic scientific paradigm. This century has already witnessed a number of major overhauls of scientific notions, namely quantum mechanics and the relativity theory.

These considerations apply, with all their strength, to finance and economics. There are many different mathematical models that compete to explain the relatively scarce empirical data. In addition, it has to be pointed out that in finance theory we are not formulating basic laws of nature, but are modeling a complex system. The no-arbitrage principle cannot be considered a basic law, as it is related to some market structure. Ultimately, finance theory is the search for an optimal model of markets.

Models are all approximate and describe data with some error, often of a significant magnitude. To compare models with empirical data, one must establish some validation procedure and select some criteria of best models. One cannot simply adopt the model that best fits data, as models fit data with many different modalities. The choice of models requires a procedure that might not be simple and straightforward, and that is subject to a conventional element.

These considerations apply, in particular, to the question of market efficiency. As markets are essentially characterized by a set of pairs of price and dividend time series, one for each security, the test of market efficiency is reduced to understanding if these data can be explained by models that respect the no-arbitrage condition. We would like to emphasize that the test of market efficiency always implies a model of the market. It does not really make sense to test "if actual prices show inefficiencies": efficiency, and more precisely no arbitrage, is a theoretically defined term.

As there are infinite possible models, the answer is not so easy, not even conceptually. Consider the following. One might test if actual data disprove a specific class of models within the limits of observational accuracy. This task has been accomplished many times. A number of observations have shown that the distribution of data and the level of forecastability present in actual markets are incompatible with certain assumptions on market dynamics.

Is this a proof of market inefficiency? One has to be careful in formulating an answer. As there are infinite possible "efficient" market models, it is no final proof of market inefficiency. Other models might be compatible with the observations. On the other hand, if all attempts to explain data with no-arbitrage models fail, one might be forced to conclude that a conceptual revision is in order. The complexity of an explanation along classical lines might, in fact, be inordinately large.

It should be noted, however, that this does not imply that markets show arbitrage opportunities. It might imply that the conceptualization based on determining a single probability distribution in the absence of operational constraints might not be appropriate and different conceptualizations might be required.

In fact, it should be clear that the discovery of arbitrage opportunities implies the existence of certainty in forecasts. There is arbitrage if some correlations are known with certainty, or at least with near certainty. The absence of arbitrage is effectively the absence of *sure* possibilities of making profit without risk. It is clear that if any such situation could be scientifically ascertained, it would be immediately exploited and would disappear.

Any eventual test of market efficiency is not a thorough test of whether agents are omniscient utility maximizers, but only if market data are compatible with some model, i.e., a set of stochastic processes that respect the no-arbitrage condition. As usual in science, what is tested is not the intuitive concept but some *theory-laden* version of it.

The conclusion seems to be that the hypothesis of market efficiency, or equivalently the no-arbitrage condition, is very robust in a conceptual setting that is based on determining a global probability distribution. In no way can certainty about future events be achieved with the present experimental and analytical tools. On the other hand, no-arbitrage models do not fit data with perfect accuracy. There are large deviations between theory and observations. To gain more explanatory power, a new conceptual framework would be needed. Despite efforts in this direction, the no-arbitrage framework remains the key conceptual framework.

16.3 Forecasting and the no-arbitrage principle

One of the hallmarks of adaptive methods is their ability to produce superior forecasts. The interest in methodologies such as chaos theory and neural networks is based on the hope that their application could result in trading strategies able to generate excess returns. Chapter 17 explores some of these technologies. First, however, we would like to put forecasting methodologies in the context of the finance theory as outlined above and to explore the meaning of earning excess returns.

Forecasting, in one way or another, is the key task of financial modeling. This fact is often misrepresented. Many describe financial modeling as sound science while forecasting is betting against the odds of the market. We engage in science because we want to predict some quantity(ies) by measuring other quantities. In particular, we want to predict future values based on present values. Our ability to produce forecasts across all sciences is not consistent and varies greatly in function of the phenomena under investigation. We are very confident that we can predict some phenomena with high accuracy while the explanation of other phenomena carries much uncertainty. This is due to a number of factors, from ignorance of basic laws to the complexity of the calculations involved.

Finance is no exception. There are a number of rules that seem quite well-founded; experimental data show only minor discrepancies with theoretical predictions. As mentioned above, this is the case, for instance, with the no-arbitrage principle. We are quite confident that predictions based on the no-arbitrage principle will be confirmed by observations. Other laws are not so robust. For instance, there is no sound theory to predict the future evolution of individual stock prices. This dichotomy of methods suggests separating that part of the theory that is "sound" from that which is more questionable. This separation is, however, largely illusory. A comprehensive view of financial phenomena is required for modeling.

To illustrate the above, recall that an economy is described by a probability space $(\Omega, \mathfrak{F}, P)$ with a filtration F and a set of dividend and price adapted processes. In discussing no-arbitrage models, we remarked that under technical conditions in complete markets there is a state-price deflator and a unique equivalent martingale measure so that prices and gains are computed through an expectation operator. Pricing relationships are restrictions expressed through the equivalent martingale measure theory.

A key feature of this model is that, in general, there are a number of independent risk factors that are priced by the market. All other securities are priced in function of these factors. In particular, these factors could be securities themselves, so that all other securities are redundant and can be priced by arbitrage, forming replicating trading strategies. Market models are thus made up of a number of independent primary dividend and price processes plus a number of derived processes priced through logical constraints.

The no-arbitrage principle is a relative valuation method insofar as it can price a security with respect to other securities. How the market prices independent risk factors is a characteristic of the market that cannot be taken into account by the no-arbitrage principle. We thus need independent models of how the fundamental prices evolve in time, i.e., we need a suitable description of the stochastic process of the fundamental prices. Note that equilibrium pricing does not solve the problem of describing the basic risk factors: it tackles the problem of asset pricing from the point of view of agents in the economy. Pricing independent factors implies an independent description of the stochastic processes that represent dividends and prices.

The key characteristic of a forecasting method is the ability to model the data generation process (DGP) of the time series to be modeled. The DGP can be understood in a deterministic or probabilistic sense. In a deterministic sense, it is a function that relates the next value to the present and past values of a time series. As there are uncertainties in any forecast, a deterministic forecast produces a path that is the best forecast. A probabilistic forecast, on the other hand, relates the probability distribution of future values to present and past values. There is a probability distribution of paths. It is, however, possible to compute expected values and other moments of the distribution.

One can conceive different models where market constraints play a stronger or weaker role in function of the number of factors. At one extreme, there are highly constrained market models in which all prices are determined by a small number of factors, even by one single factor. The classic CAPM is an example of a market that is described by a single factor. At the other extreme, there are market models in which every security is an independent price process. Mathematically, these conditions are relatively easy to determine in a discrete setting where there are only a finite number of securities and a finite number of trading moments. They might be much harder to formulate in a continuous-time setting.

The objective of finance theory is to find the models that best fit data and thus the best combination of forecasting algorithms and the description of market constraints. It should be clear that forecasting methodologies play a vital role in modeling, even in the no-arbitrage setting, as they model the basic factors.

16.4 Is it possible to earn excess returns?

The notion of excess returns, in simple terms, means that the financial markets offer different opportunities for return depending on an agent's knowledge and shrewdness. In a sense, the quest for maximum returns is what finance is all about. When one tries to make the above notion precise, however, it becomes somewhat blurred. The key point is: How do we know what kind of return opportunities financial markets offer?

To answer this question, some theory is required. This is a recurring theme: to make evaluations, we need a theory. One might gain a first simple measurement of effective returns by taking the returns averaged over a large portfolio of securities. One might be tempted to say that the above measure is an indication of the total ability of the economy to produce wealth. In a sense it is. However, it is clear that the combined action of agents plays a role in pushing prices up or down. As a result, the global return from the market is a question, not only of the ability of the economy to produce a stream of dividends, but also of the reaction of financial markets.

One might actually compute the average over large portfolios and evaluate their probability distribution. If one takes sub-portfolios, however, one would almost certainly get different results of the distribution of returns with respect to a broad index. One is tempted to take as a reference not the return on a broad average portfolio, but the return consequent to some optimal trading strategy. To define this type of measure, a model of the market is necessary. Given a model of the market — a system of price and dividend adapted processes — one can define optimal strategies. It should be remarked that there is no single optimal trading strategy. Each agent has his or her own model of optimality that embodies his or her own optimal trade-off between risk and return.

It is clear that if an agent wants to evaluate the theoretical returns of the market, he or she has to solve a twofold problem: 1) the choice of the optimal model, and 2) the choice of the optimal trading strategy consequent to that model. The choice is not unique, as every model is only approximate and implements a compromise between different modeling issues. The choice between models also implies a trade-off between the ability to forecast risk factors, i.e., to model the DGP of factor processes, and market constraints. It should be noted that this choice is possible, even within the no-arbitrage framework.

In general, different models will induce different optimal trading strategies, even assuming the same model for agent optimality. Implementing different strategies will generate different returns. To compare these returns, one needs to know their risk profile. But their risk profile depends on the model chosen. Thus comparing returns of trading strategies from different models might be a theoretically challenging task.

The above illustrates the conceptual difficulties in understanding what returns are theoretically possible in a certain market and how it could eventually be possible to improve over these evaluations. In practice, some portfolio and some trading strategy is taken as a benchmark against which performance is measured. One runs a trading strategy for a sufficiently long time and then compares the returns and variance generated with those of the benchmark. Variations of this concept have, in fact, been formalized in what is known as the RaROC (risk-adjusted return on capital).

In all practical cases, the ability to generate excess returns is evaluated by comparing return and variance of a specific trading strategy against some benchmark or eventually against some theoretical model. An important case arises when an agent has adopted a model in which he or she is reasonably confident but for which a number of discrepancies with actual observations have been found. The agent might maintain that the model is a faithful description of the market and that the discrepancies are market "mispricings" that will be corrected later. He or she can then exploit this situation to earn a return in excess of what would be possible within the limits of the model.

A different situation arises with forecasting tools. With the diffusion of deterministic forecasting methods such as neural networks — but also with less sophisticated tools such as technical analysis — one has a sort of mechanical trading strategy. The question is how to evaluate the performance of this forecasting/ trading system.

A deterministic forecasting tool might give the illusion of finding arbitrage opportunities, as it projects into the future price differentials that allow for gains. Given a deterministic forecasting methodology, one can find many profitable strategies. Suppose that one has a forecasting methodology and that, in consequence, he or she defines a trading strategy that generates a certain return. Suppose, for simplicity, that only stocks are traded and that there are no transaction costs to take into account. One can obviously track returns over different periods and compare them with the returns generated by various portfolios of stocks. One can thus evaluate the average return and the average volatility and compare this risk/return profile with that of other portfolios. Apparently, in this way, one might effectively find discrepancies that seem to show high returns.

These considerations have been a major problem in the application of forecasting methodologies. First, we do not really know the risk profile of a forecasting methodology. Sure, it is possible to compute variances of past returns and even higher-order moments, but these measures might be largely insufficient if the *model risk* of the forecasting algorithm has some strange shape. The key problem is that the uncertainty associated with the forecast is not known. What might look like a highly profitable strategy might, in effect, be a risky scheme that could produce substantial losses.

References

Cherubini, U., "Fuzzy Measures and Asset Prices," Banca Commerciale Italiana, Milan, April 1994.

Dalang, R.C., A. Morton and W. Willenger, "Equivalent Martingale Measures and No-Arbitrage in Stochastic Securities Market Models," *Stochastics and Stochastics Reports*, 29: 185-201, 1990.

Delbaen, F., "Representing Martingale Measures When Asset Prices Are Continuous and Bounded," *Mathematical Finance*, 2 (2): 107-130, 1992.

Epstein, L.G., "Consumption, Savings, and Asset Returns with Non-expected Utility," *Workshop on Decision Theory and Economic Laboratory*, ISER, University of Siena, July 1995.

Epstein, L.G. and T. Wang, "Intertemporal Asset Pricing Under Knightian Uncertainty," *Econometrica*, 62: 283-322, 1994.

Jarrow, R.A. and D.B. Madan, "Valuing and Hedging Contingent Claims on Semimartingales," Johnson Graduate School of Management, Cornell University, Ithaca, NY, December 1995.

17. Adaptive Computational Methods

17.1 The data-rich approach to science

There is a new approach to science in which knowledge is discovered with methods based on the processing of large amounts of data. This is a truly scientific approach, different from, though complementary to, the classical theoretical approach. The latter is founded on describing physical phenomena in a mathematical language. Theories are constructed as axiomatic systems where knowledge is embodied in a small number of concise statements called axioms. All detailed physical knowledge can be derived, as a logical consequence, from these axioms plus descriptive hypotheses.

The recognition that mathematics is an effective way of describing nature was in itself a major scientific achievement. The physicist Eugene Wigner referred to the "unreasonable effectiveness" of mathematics in describing nature. It is not difficult to grasp this wonder. We try to describe the apparently enormous complexity of nature with a mathematical language that ultimately has a very simple formulation, reconstructing the original complexity through a chain of simple operations.

Although the axiomatic approach led to the development of a nearly complete science, it cannot account for a full description of the complexity of natural and artificial phenomena. This happens not because fundamental laws are violated, but because it is desirable to understand the evolution of structures that are intrinsically complex. Relating the behavior of complex structures to basic laws would require an impossibly long and complex chain of logical relations. There might be more subtle reasons that make it impossible to describe the behavior of complex structures in terms of basic physical laws, reasons, for instance, related to quantum indeterminacy that cannot be averaged away in complex structures. Regardless of these more subtle considerations, there are complex phenomena that simply require a large amount of information for their description. A human being or an economy is a complex structure whose behavior cannot be properly described through the standard techniques of mathematical physics.

To understand the behavior of complex structures, an information-processing approach to science has been developed. In this approach, natural objects, artifacts, and phenomena are described as *discrete* structures whose laws can be expressed as computational procedures. The underlying assumption is that there is a level of knowledge that it is possible to acquire about these systems and that that knowledge can be encoded as digital information. Whatever additional complexity there might be below this level of aggregation, it is irrelevant for the behavior of the structure as described. For example, the behavior of a computer when properly functioning can be described in purely computational terms and the fine details of its electronic components are irrelevant. The computational description of a computer is, however, no longer valid in the case of machine fault.

Computational models are generally derived from theories. To solve problems where no mathematical theory exists, however, requires a new approach to science. This approach consists in using computers to explore a large space of general approximate models, choosing the optimal one according to some defined criteria. It might well be that this process will help to distill axiomatic simple rules. Its usefulness, however, consists in dropping the requirement of simple all-encompassing models, replacing them with complex partial models. Many of these applications can be found in domains related to finance and business where the theoretical base is poor by the standards of contemporary science. However, technological domains such as the analysis of satellite data use the same approach.

There are now two distinct approaches to science: a theory-rich approach based on mathematical formulations in line with mathematical physics, and a data-rich approach based on computational methodologies independent of underlying theoretical formulations. The data-rich approach is, ultimately, a chapter in automatic science, as models — and thus scientific descriptions — are built automatically through adaptive procedures. The techniques used in building models are broadly referred to as machine learning.

17.2 Basic notions in machine learning

There are two fundamental distinctions in machine learning. The first is between supervised and unsupervised learning, the second between symbolic and non-symbolic learning.

In supervised learning, the learning system is presented with a number of successful examples and it learns from them. A typical example of supervised learning is the backpropagation training of feedforward neural networks, where the weights of the neural network are changed through the backpropagation procedure on the presentation of teaching patterns.

In non-symbolic supervised learning, what is learned is basically a numerical function. A learning system builds a representation of a numerical function upon presentation of a set of examples. As such, a learning system generalizes from known examples of a function to the entire function, and is called a generalizer. The definition of a non-symbolic generalizer is the following:

A generalizer is a system that is able to reconstruct a function $F(x)$, from R^n to R^m upon presentation of a set of p examples of the function, i.e., a set of p couples x_i, y_i, where $y_i=F(x_i)$, $i=1,p$. The set of examples is called the training set.

In finance, an important instance of generalization is forecasting: all the known cases are in the past, while generalization looks to the future.

A generalizer works assuming that the data to analyze possess some structure that can be reproduced within certain approximation limits by the models, i.e., the functions, implemented by the generalizer. In addition, it assumes that the training set contains enough information to specify all the free parameters contained in the model to be built. As there is no theoretical assurance that a generalizer will work, there is no theoretical assurance that a generalizer can effectively learn and generalize any arbitrary pattern. Otherwise put, there are many more patterns than possible generalizers.

The use of machine-learning techniques to build classifiers and generalizers rests on the assumption that natural or artificial phenomena can actually be described mathematically. When exploring a sample, one assumes that the phenomena under investigation show a certain regularity that can be described mathematically. Without this assumption, there would be no science. The problem of generalization is thus the problem of understanding the complexity of the mathematical description of phenomena and whether enough information is available to build a description.

Supervised learning is by no means constrained to numerical functions. Based on examples, machines can learn how to increase knowledge expressed through symbolic expressions. Examples of supervised symbolic learning include case-based learning. The general principle of symbolic learning is to construct and modify symbolic expressions that best fit a number of examples. To reach this goal, one has to define some way to generate and transform expressions in a given language and to test their effectiveness on known examples.

Contrary to supervised learning, unsupervised learning does not require a teaching set; the learning system evolves according to its internal dynamics and structure. In non-symbolic unsupervised learning, systems produce patterns as numerical functions. Examples include neural networks with feedback, such as the Hopfield nets. In these cases, the system starts with some input or no input at all, and evolves autonomously towards a stable state. Unsupervised learning automatically generalizes over the entire data set. In symbolic unsupervised learning, sets of rules or descriptions evolve autonomously towards some final stage. For instance, a system of relations among members of a set might evolve into the description of the partitioning of the data set according to the rules.

Unsupervised learning can be thought of as a way of developing and making explicit some type of implicit description of the system. At the start of the learning process, one does not know how the system will evolve in time. The description of the structure is unveiled during the learning process. In clustering simulation paths according to similarities, for instance, what is known at the beginning is the statement of the clustering relationships; the actual clustering becomes explicit only at the end of the process.

17.3 Genetic algorithms

Genetic algorithms (GAs) belong to a vast class of statistical optimization algorithms. GAs are, however, more than optimization algorithms. They are generalized problem-solving methodologies based on evolution strategies. They can be used — and are used — as optimization devices but, conceptually, the scope of their action is much broader.

GAs were conceived in the 1960s by John Holland at the University of Michigan. The original motivation behind their development was to capture and exploit the abstract logic of biological genetic evolution. Biological evolution has apparently been successful in evolving species highly adapted to the most diverse environmental conditions. Were it possible to abstract the logic of evolution, it was believed that this knowledge could be used to create programs that automatically produce solutions adapted to various tasks.

Following this line of thought, Holland defined algorithmic structures that showed remarkable properties of optimization and problem-solving through evolution. He called these structures genetic algorithms. GAs are now widely used in engineering applications, mostly as optimization algorithms, without excessive emphasis on their "genetic" origin.

It should be remarked that although the notion of mimicking evolution was a powerful idea, it is not in itself a strong mathematical argument, for many reasons. First, we do not really know how successful evolution is. Some of the species produced by evolution seem well-adapted to their environment according to some criteria, but the price of adaptation is high according to other criteria. Nor can we be certain that better solutions could not exist. In addition, GAs imply several idealizations of the genetic evolutionary process that might be a significant departure from a faithful account of biological evolution. It was a powerful logical intuition that evolution could be schematized in algorithms that are effective optimization devices.

The functioning of GAs is based on evolving a population of potential solutions to a problem, trying to improve their fitness as measured by some function. This scheme differentiates GAs from other optimization techniques where a single solution follows an optimization path. In the hill-climbing method, for instance, the optimization algorithm makes one solution move towards the highest point of the hill following a certain path.

GAs work on a population of individuals called chromosomes. Chromosomes are sequences of binary digits, i.e., sequences of 0s and 1s. Each digit is called a gene. The terminology of genes and chromosomes is standard in the literature, so we will adhere to it. It goes back to the origin of GAs as the abstract modeling of biological evolution.

In practical applications of GAs, each chromosome represents a possible solution to a given problem. GAs are thus applicable to problems whose solutions can be encoded as strings of bits. Although this might seem an important limitation, in practice most problems can be easily encoded in this language. From a theoretical standpoint, any problem that can be expressed as a finite set of expressions can be encoded as a string of bits. Encoding is therefore not a fundamental theoretical limitation.

The population of chromosomes evolves following the action of a reproduction operator and of two genetic operators that mimic reproduction and genetic mutation called, respectively, the cross-over operator and the mutation operator. The sequence of operations of GAs is the following. Assuming that time advances in discrete incremental steps, let $P(t_i)$ be the population at time step t_i, so that $P(t_{i+1})$ is the population at time step t_{i+1}. Operators are applied in sequence at each time step. Starting from the initial population, a new population is created through the action of the reproduction operator. The reproduction operator creates a new population selecting individuals with probabilities proportional to their fitness value. The new population has a higher fitness level.

A certain fraction of the new population is then selected for mating and mutation through the action of the genetic operators' cross-over and mutation. Schematically, the process is as follows:

$P(t_i)$ population at time t_i
      reproduction
      cross-over
      mutation
$P(t_{i+1})$ population at time t_{i+1}.

Let's now take a closer look at each step.

First, the notion of the fitness function has to be introduced. The fitness function is a numerical function defined over the entire set I of possible individuals, i.e., of admissible chromosomes:

$$F(x), x \epsilon I, I \text{ set of possible chromosomes.}$$

In binary representation, this poses no problem, as any string is an admissible chromosome. The fitness function is a measure of the fitness, according to some criteria, of each individual that belongs to the population. The fitness function is a key concept in GAs: it is a quantitative measure of the "goodness" of a solution. In optimization problems, the fitness function might coincide with the goal function to be maximized or minimized. However, this is not necessarily the case. The goal function can be modified, for instance, to include constraints in the fitness function. In general problem-solving, the fitness function has to be created as an *ad-hoc* representation of the problem's goal.

During the reproduction phase, a new population of the same size is created, choosing individuals with probabilities proportional to their fitness. The reproduction procedure could be as follows, where, to avoid notational clutter, x represents a generic chromosome in a certain ordering, for example, the decimal value of the string of bits that represent that chromosome:

1) The total fitness of the population, F, is computed as the sum of the fitness of every individual:

$$F = \Sigma F(x), \; x \epsilon I.$$

2) A probability, $p(x)$, is computed for every chromosome $x \epsilon I$ as the rate between the individual fitness and the total fitness.
3) A cumulative probability, $P(x)$, is computed for every chromosome x as the sum of probabilities $p(y)$ of chromosomes y that come before x in the selected ordering:

$$P(x) = \Sigma p(y), \; y \; precedes \; x.$$

The selection mechanism consists in generating, for each x, a random number r in the interval $(0,1)$, and selecting the chromosome x such that $P(x-1)<r\leq P(x)$. This is a roulette wheel type of mechanism with slots of a size proportional to the probability of selection.

If the population size is N, this process is repeated N times until a new population of the same size as the original is created. In general, this new population will have a different composition than the original population, because, on average, the fittest individuals will be selected more than once and the least fit will not be selected at all. This process is the abstract representation of the process of the survival of the fittest hypothesized in biological evolution.

After reproduction, the new population is subject to the action of the cross-over and mutation operators. The cross-over operator represents the mechanism of transmission of genetic information in reproduction. In its simplest formulation, one-point uniform cross-over, two chromosomes are divided into two complementary portions that are exchanged as shown in Figure 2.

Cross-over is a probabilistic operator, as only a fraction of the population randomly chosen undergoes cross-over. The fraction of the population that undergoes cross-over, p_c, is a design parameter of the algorithm. The process of selection is as follows. After selecting the parameter p_c, probability of cross-over, a random number r is generated for each chromosome x. The chromosome x is selected if $r < p_c$. This process is repeated for each chromosome in the population so that an average number of $p_c N$ chromosomes, where N is the size of the population, is selected. As it is necessary to select an even number of chromosomes, it might be necessary to add or delete one chromosome if, at the end of the

Figure 2
Parts of strings are exchanged. Strings are selected at random for crossover

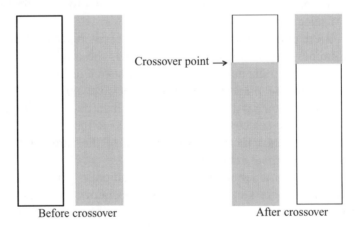

Before crossover   After crossover

process, an odd number of chromosomes remains.

The chromosomes selected for cross-over are then randomly paired and, for each pair, a random number p in the range $(0,$ length of chromosomes) is generated. This number is the cross-over point. Two new chromosomes are generated, exchanging the portions above and below the point p in the old chromosomes. The new chromosomes replace the old ones in the population.

While the cross-over operator exchanges information between two existing chromosomes, the mutation operator is intended to introduce novel information that will be tested under the process of selection. The mutation operator acts on a bit-by-bit basis. A probability of mutation, p_n, is selected as one of the parameters of the algorithm. A random number r in the range $(0,1)$ is generated for each gene, i.e., for each bit in each string that makes the chromosomes. The gene is mutated, i.e., its value is reversed, if $r<p_n$.

The sequential application of the reproduction, cross-over, and mutation operators is the evolution cycle of genetic algorithms. At the end of the cycle, the fitness function is again evaluated and it is decided if a new cycle should be run. How to decide when to stop is a critical issue. As there is no convergence theorem for GAs, there is no assurance that in some sense the fitness values will converge. Stopping criteria can be a decision on the number of iterations to be performed, or some heuristic measure of convergence of fitness values.

Why do GAs work? There is no rigorous mathematical theory to predict if and when evolution will evolve towards optimal values of the fitness function. Presently there is a lot of research on the theory of GAs. It is aimed at understanding why GAs work and under what conditions. The theoretical work is supported by experimental work — both in research and in business applications — that shows that GAs are effective optimization algorithms capable of outperforming other algorithms. In particular,

GAs work well in complex optimization problems with many local maxima and minima. They are apparently able to avoid the problem of getting stuck in local optima, a problem typical of most optimization algorithms.

Since their original conception, many different versions of GAs have been advanced. While the general scheme remains the same, various problem representations and genetic operators have been proposed. As regards representation, the binary coding of chromosomes is convenient mathematically, but might prove cumbersome practically. A more general floating point representation, in which a chromosome is a string of floating point numbers, has been proposed. To use floating point numbers, operators — in particular the mutation operator — must be adapted. Mutation, for instance, does not simply flip a binary digit but generates a new random number.

One problem with floating point representations is that operators might not produce admissible individuals, creating the need to constrain the operators to search only in the space of possible chromosomes. This can be achieved in a number of ways, for instance modifying the fitness function with a penalty term that makes it practically impossible to search the space of "illegal" individuals. The same technique can be used in general to handle constraints in optimization problems.

Many new specialized genetic operators have been proposed. The objective of these reformulations of GAs is to make them more suitable for the solution of specific problems where it is possible to use some *a priori* knowledge.

How are GAs used? The first important application of GAs is to find maxima or minima of numerical functions. To illustrate this application, consider the case of a single-variable function $y = F(x)$, where x can vary in the interval (a,b). The problem is to find the global maximum or minimum of F in the range (a,b).

The application of GAs is rather straightforward. If a binary representation is used, chromosomes are simply the binary representations of values of x in the range (a,b). The length of chromosomes clearly depends on the precision that is desired. At each step, the population is a set of values of x, and their corresponding fitness is the value of $F(x)$. Following evolution, potential solutions, i.e., sets of x values, distribute over the most promising areas where maxima or minima are most likely to be found.

There is no natural way to use floating representation for univariate problems. However, if the function to be optimized is a function of N variables, $y=F(x_1,...,x_N)$, it is natural to take as a chromosome a vector of x_i, $i=1,N$ floating point numbers.

One of the most innovative applications of GAs is genetic programming, invented by John Koza at Stanford University. Genetic programming is based on the notion that programs can be encoded as strings of digits and that the "goodness" of a program can be expressed as a numerical function. This idea was originally applied by Koza to LISP programs. Similar implementations include the evolution of neural networks and other types of algorithms.

17.4 Neural networks

The following paragraphs look at neural networks and their functioning. There are a large variety of network architectures, topologies, functioning, and training schemes. NeuralWare, a Pittsburgh, Pennsylvania-based supplier of neural software, offers 28 different types of networks, plus many different training algorithms. Neural networks are electronic devices able to perform a number of well-defined logical tasks. They are more complex than, for example, amplifiers or filters, but there is no reason why their behavior cannot be specified in functional terms.

This perspective is fundamental for the maturing of the neural network technology. Technology matures in a certain field when it can adopt a black-box approach, where devices are characterized by their functional specifications and by a set of characteristics that can be related to functions. The different options of neural networks correspond to different functional specifications of their behavior. There is not yet a complete functional characterization of neural networks, but this is the direction in which technology is moving.

Neural networks are conceptually simple computational structures that originated from the effort to understand intelligent behavior from the physical structure of the human brain. In 1947, Warren McCulloch and Walter Pitts proposed a mathematical model of nerve cells. Their model is a simple unit that receives as input numerical values from other units, multiplies each input times a weighting factor, and computes an output value through a threshold function. As nerve cells are called neurons, this system is called an artificial neuron, or simply a neuron when there is no risk of confusion with a physical nerve cell. A scheme of an artificial neuron is shown below in Figure 3.

Figure 3
Representation of an artificial neuron

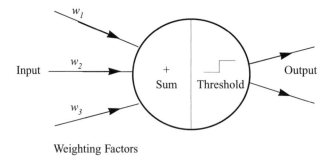

Weighting Factors

In their monumental work, McCulloch and Pitts were able to prove that a computational structure made up of neurons of this type has a number of interesting properties and can execute complex computations, including the predicate logic.

In the 1950s, Frank Rosemblatt built networks called Perceptrons, made of a single layer of neurons. He demonstrated that a Perceptron could learn any pattern that it could be programmed to recognize. This was a rather remarkable result. There was a lot of excitement about Perceptrons and many experiments were carried out. It was experimentally confirmed that Percep-trons could indeed learn many patterns, but at the same time there seemed to be patterns that a Perceptron could not learn.

In 1969, MIT's Marvin Minsky and Seymour Papert wrote their famous book, *Perceptrons*, in which they demonstrated that there were patterns that Perceptrons could not learn. Among the impossible patterns were simple logical structures such as exclusive OR. This book is credited with having virtually stopped research on neural networks for nearly two decades, though many other factors were probably responsible for the fall-off of the interest in neural networks in the 1970s and the first half of the 1980s.

In the second half of the 1980s, there was a rebirth of research in neural networks that started at MIT with David Rumelhart, James McClelland, and the PDP group. They showed that neural networks with hidden layers do not have the limitations of single-layer Perceptrons. In fact, multilayer networks could learn virtually any pattern. Rumelhart rediscovered independently the back-propagation training rule that proved to be very useful in training neural networks. Following the publication by Rumelhart, McClelland, and the PDP group of *Parallel Distributed Processing*, a book that was to become the manifesto of connectionism, there was an explosion of research on neural networks.

A good deal of research is devoted to exploring the capabilities of neural networks as a general cognitive paradigm, or at least as an element of a cognitive paradigm. An even larger portion of research has been devoted to the practical usage of neural networks. The ability of neural networks to be trained and the fact that they are universal function approximators has opened the way to a wealth of advanced technological implementations. It is fair to say that whatever place neural networks will retain in the theory of cognition, they are firmly established as a technological device with many interesting applications.

A neural network is an assembly of computational units, called neurons, with a pattern of connections. A number of neurons receive input from the outside and are called input neurons, while other neurons produce output values.

The general structure of a neuron is shown earlier in Figure 3. A neuron receives as input a set of numerical values, each multiplied by a constant called a "weight." The input neurons receive input from the outside without any processing. The remaining neurons receive input from other neurons. If there are N neurons in a network, numbered through an index $j=1,N$, w_{ij} is the weight that multiplies the value that propagates from neuron i to neuron j. Thus the structure of the net is described by a matrix of $N{\times}N$ weights w_{ij}.

The sum of the weighted inputs to a neuron is then passed through a threshold function:

$F(x)=1$ *if* $x{\geq}$*threshold value,* $F(x)=0$ *if* $x{<}$*threshold value.*

A neuron outputs a value which is *0* or *1* according to whether the sum of its weighted inputs is above or below the threshold value. The threshold in the function F can be simply *0*, as a different threshold value can be implemented adding a fixed input.

The function F as defined above is a discontinuous non-differentiable function. It can be replaced by a sigmoidal function that is mathematically more tractable. It should be remarked that neurons, as defined above, are highly idealized structures quite remote from the actual behavior of a physical neuron.

A network is described by the matrix of the weights, by the topology of its connections, and by the transfer function of its neurons. To complete the description of a network, the timing of the updating of neurons has to be specified. In neural networks, there is a time lag between the presentation of input signals and the firing of output signals. In biological neurons, the time lag between input and output reflects the internal chemico-physical behavior of the neuron. In artificial neural networks, it is an idealization that is theoretically important, as it is responsible for the evolution of networks with feedback.

In general, at any given time step, the input and output values do not necessarily reflect the function F, as values may or may not be updated. There are two fundamental updating modes, synchronous and asynchronous.

In the synchronous updating mode, all neurons are updated at a given time step. This mode implies a central timing and a central control that gives the order to update. When the order is issued, each neuron updates its output value according to the sigmoidal rule. Its output will eventually change and the new value will be used by all neurons to which it is connected in the next step.

In the asynchronous mode, the updating is essentially random: at each instant, neurons to update are chosen by chance. Alternatively, each neuron has a fixed probability of updating for each interval of time. The two approaches are equivalent.

One can look at neural networks as generalized computational structures made up of simple computing elements with a network of interconnections. Although neural networks are simple mathematical structures, their apparent simplicity is deceptive: they might show highly complex patterns of behavior. There are many different types of network structures and correlated behavior. There are also different ways to look at the behavior of networks.

First, it is important to distinguish between networks that operate in unsupervised and supervised learning modes, or eventually in a hybrid mode. In the unsupervised mode, a network evolves according to its own internal dynamics. The structure of the network and the weights might remain constant or they can be adapted to their own evolution. The topology of networks that work in an unsupervised mode must have some kind of feedback to allow for the network to show interesting dynamic behavior. The feedback might be provided by the network itself or by some more complex arrangement through which the output is fed to some external device and then back into the original network.

In the supervised learning mode, a neural network receives input as a number of patterns with corresponding target output patterns. The topology and the weights of the network are then adjusted to make the network's output as close as possible to the target outputs according to some metric. The adjustment of topology and weights is done by computational procedures such as backpropagation, separate from the network. It is also possible to combine supervised and unsupervised learning in networks that have their own internal dynamic but whose weights and topology are adjusted in function of the target output.

The activity of a network can be described by saying that a network computes a set of mappings $y=(x)$, where x and y are vectors in the input and output spaces. In supervised learning the mapping is learned from a set of examples, while in unsupervised learning the mapping is discovered by the system's dynamics.

How can these processes be mathematically described? One general framework for a global analysis of neural networks is statistical mechanics. Supervised learning is a process of mapping approximation. As such, it is essentially a problem of the optimization of a cost function. However, as the interesting function is not the approximation to a known function, but the generalization to a set of unknown functions within certain error limits, statistics is a natural framework. Unsupervised learning can be cast in the framework of statistical mechanics and information theory.

Another important perspective is the theory of dynamic systems. In this framework, neural networks are seen as dynamic systems that evolve following certain paths that can be studied by the theory of non-linear dynamic systems.

Feedforward neural networks

Feedforward neural networks are perhaps the most widely diffused networks in industrial applications. Their popularity comes from their ability to work as universal function approximators when used in connection with suitable training procedures such as backpropagation. The structure of a feedforward neural network is shown in Figure 4.

In a feedforward network, the first layer simply dispatches input values to the following layers. As a matter of terminology, the present tendency is to consider this as the first layer. The first layer is called the "input layer," the last layer is called the "output layer," and those in between, as they do not have any contact with the outside, are called "hidden layers."

Each layer of neurons receives inputs only from the layer immediately preceding it and outputs only to the layer immedi-

Figure 4
A feedforward neural network

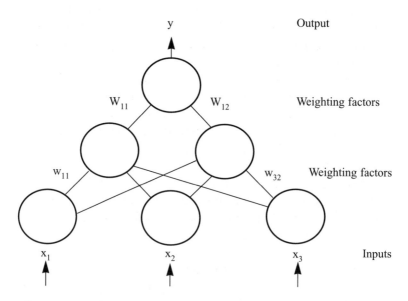

ately following it. This network topology is called feedforward because values propagate forward in the network; there is no feedback from one layer to the previous ones. The only feedback to the network is provided by the training procedure during the learning phase. When the network operates, the propagation of values is strictly forward.

The use of feedforward neural networks in engineering applications is based on the fact that they are universal function approximators and are trainable on sample data. In 1988, G. Cybenko demonstrated that a feedforward network with at least two hidden layers is a universal function approximator in the sense that it implements a function from the input values to the

output values that can come arbitrarily close to any function provided that a sufficient number of nodes is available and that the
weights are appropriately chosen.

Although Cybenko's result was proved only recently, with some
hindsight it should not come as a surprise. Consider, for instance,
the output of a node of a single-layer network. It can be written as:

$$F(x) = \Sigma w_{ij} . f_j(x).$$

where the f_j are the transfer functions of each node. The output of
a network with a hidden layer can be represented easily as a sum
of products of functions f_j.

In general, the output of a network can always be written as
the sum of a set of fundamental functions, each multiplied by a
factor. It is a well-known mathematical technique to represent a
function as a sum of basis functions, where the basis functions
span the entire set of possible functions under suitable conditions.
Truncating expansions after a finite number of terms gives an
approximation of the target function. Well-known examples are
the expansion of a function in a Taylor series of power or the
expansion in a Fourier series of sine or cosine functions.

In the above cases, basis functions obey fundamental properties such as orthogonality that make them attractive from the
point of view of the analytical description of coefficients. Neural
networks use functions that do not implement an orthogonal basis
but that, nonetheless, can approximate any function.

The proof that neural networks are universal function approximators ensures that there are no intrinsic limitations to the type
of functions that the networks can generalize. It does not, however, specify how to construct a neural network that actually performs the generalizing task. In other words, the proof ensures that
there are neural networks that come arbitrarily close to the func-

tions that we might want to approximate, but it does not say how to build them. To build a network that approximates a certain function, a training algorithm is needed. The desired neural network is thus built through a learning process. The problem is one of linking a training procedure to the functional specification of training goals.

One training goal is to make the network mimic the samples. This is an important goal; often behavior can be easily shown but its description in logical steps might be cumbersome or difficult. An example is the recognition of shapes that are well-defined and stable, such as signatures on checks or contracts. In these cases, the fact that a neural network is a universal function approximator ensures that a solution exists and the training procedure can be cast in the framework of a functional specification of the training goals.

The training scheme can, in fact, be described as an optimization problem where the function to be optimized reaches well-defined maxima or minima on the output to be produced or the input to be recognized. In these cases, going from a functional statement of the problem to a training scheme based on minimization of cost functions is straightforward, at least conceptually. It is, however, important to note the complexity of the task that can be learned, a complexity that might exceed the human capacity to specify the task in logical terms.

A broader learning goal is to generalize from a selected set of inputs for which the response pattern is known to the entire set of possible inputs. There are several possible training strategies. One is to keep the network dimensionality low. This means that only the most important features of behavior are considered; details are ignored. If the dimensionality of a network (i.e., the number of weights as free parameters) is high, the network might simply fit noise, leading to poor generalization. This is known as over-fitting. If, however, the number of parameters is low, the training procedure is forced to fit only the global features.

Determining the size and topology of the network is a key consideration. It might be possible to use theoretical considerations that prescribe the size of the networks to be used. Alternatively, networks of different sizes might be tried. One could start with a low-dimensionality network and increase the dimensionality, verifying performance improvements, or one could start with a high-dimensionality network and reduce its size progressively. Both techniques involve questions on the use of training and test data.

An alternative strategy for generalization is to impose constraints that limit the network's fitting noise by constraining the type of optimization goals to achieve. In this case, the training algorithm does not simply try to come as close as possible to the samples, but optimizes a more complex function that includes a measure of the distance from the samples as well as other terms. A possible approach, for instance, is to maximize the information gain with the addition of new inputs.

In summary, a framework for learning should include three elements: a description of the complexity of the phenomena to be described, an adequate training set, and the generalizing abilities related to the structure of the neural network.

17.5 Induction trees

Neural networks produce predictions and classifications expressed in the language of mathematical formulas. The basic output of a neural network is a function whose generalization ability can be understood and checked by a human operator only through the use of validation procedures. A neural network captures correlations between values and slopes of the training function through a process of function approximation that is not intuitive.

In business applications, however, it is often desirable to grasp immediately, in intuitive terms, what the system is doing. There are several reasons for this. One is the desire to verify and check the work of the system, to offer explanations. But perhaps the most important is the need to build confidence in the technologies.

A number of machine-learning algorithms discover patterns and structures in ways that are understandable to human observers. They achieve this goal by essentially performing a number of tests in succession. Each test is a question on the structure of the data to be explored. Its answers depend on how data are effectively organized so that patterns are learned from the data.

As cascades of tests can be represented as trees, these methods are generally referred to as identification or induction trees. The end product of building a tree can be a set of rules or a set of partitions that give structure to a set of data. To some extent, rules and partitions can translate into each other, so the two formulations, although not equivalent, have much in common.

Trees can be built either in supervised or unsupervised learning modes. In supervised learning, a set of samples with a known classification is used to build rules that are then applied to the entire data set. In the unsupervised mode, tests regard the global distribution of data on the entire set.

Identification trees are the most widely diffused machine-learning algorithms in data mining. They were independently discovered by statisticians and by the artificial intelligence (AI) community. In the AI community, the prototype of induction trees is the ID3 family of systems developed by Ross Quinlan. Statisticians Breiman and others developed a similar approach called Classification And Regression Trees (CART).

To understand how identification trees work, suppose that a set of samples with appropriate classifications is given. This means that there is a set of sample individuals, each characterized by a set of values of some features, and that to each individual corresponds a classification value. Suppose, for instance, that we want to estimate how interest rates will vary in function of a number of parameters, e.g., money supply, inflation rate, GNP, and unemployment index. From past experience, the interest rate corresponding to some set of these four parameters is known. The problem is to find a set of rules to predict interest rates for any set of values of the parameters.

Before proceeding further, it is appropriate to remark that this problem corresponds to reconstructing a function of four variables given a number of sample points, with the additional limitation that function values are constrained to the number of fixed values that are to be found in the samples. It should be remarked that the number of possible combinations of the input parameters is already high for even a limited number of possible values of input parameters. Suppose there are twenty values for each possible input variable; the number of combinations is 20^4, or 160,000 possible combinations.

This observation makes clear that it is generally impossible to solve these problems by creating a direct look-up table, as the number of entries is enormous. If it were possible to perform experiments, a well-known strategy in experimental physics would suggest planning a series of experiments where all variables but one are kept constant. In this way, one could create a regular partition of the feature space with each experiment representative of a partition. It would then be easy to derive classification rules, simply grouping together all the sets with identical classification. This, however, is not possible, as only historical data are available.

If one would attempt the same regular partitioning with historical data, he or she would face two types of problems. First, partitions might contain data with different classifications, making it impossible to assign a classification to that partition. Second, a number of partitions might be completely empty. Identification trees are strategies for finding the partitions where historical data assume the same value or where their range is the smallest possible.

From the point of view of data mining and analysis, function approximators such as neural networks and identification trees have complementary goals. Function approximators reconstruct a function so that they can answer questions on the value that a function assumes on arbitrary points, while identification trees reconstruct the set on which a function assumes a certain value. Identification trees can work as generalizers with techniques to assign points to partitions.

What is the search strategy of an identification tree? There are many different strategies that depend basically on three parameters: what are the features and how many to consider, the order in which features are selected and the tests applied, and how to optimize the partitioning at each test. At one extreme, there are only binary features; at the other extreme, there are continuous variables for which the optimal partitioning point needs to be decided.

Different strategies give different results, because at the end of the induction process the partitions might be more or less homogeneous. A perfectly homogeneous partition, i.e., one that contains only one classification value for each partition set, shows an apparent 0 classification error. In general, the apparent error will be proportional to the homogeneity of the classification. However, a very small or zero apparent error rate is not a guarantee of good generalization properties, as was the case with neural networks.

In the case of binary features, there is no possibility of choosing an optimal cutting point and the choice is limited to the length of the tree, i.e., the number of variables and the order in which variables are taken. Due to the computational costs involved, one cannot explore all possible trees and choose the best; some heuristics must be used. One common heuristic is to order the variables according to their classification ability. The induction procedure starts by selecting the feature, i.e., the variable, that partitions into sets of maximum homogeneity. A measure of homogeneity is supplied by information theory concepts, such as the amount of information in each set. The same test applies at each successive node. The process stops when there are either no more variables or no more samples.

Continuous variables present more difficult problems, as for each variable one has to decide the optimal cut. This is a difficult optimization problem that can be solved with the use of, for example, genetic algorithms. There are many examples of partitioning sets using GAs as optimization devices for rule selection.

If partitioning is achieved by cutting hyper-rectangles in the feature space, there are straightforward procedures for creating sets of production rules that translate partitions into an English-like language. When induction trees are used in applications such as the prediction of interest rates, this is a real advantage. When trees are built from very large samples with a rich feature space, the advantage of plain rules can be more illusory than real.

In summary, induction trees perform tasks similar to those of neural networks. Their main advantage is that their output can be cast in the form of a set of understandable rules. There are a large number of possible implementations of decision trees and related algorithms. They are subject to the same considerations already made for neural networks.

17.6 Hybridization techniques
A recent but important development in machine learning is

the use of hybrid systems that combine more than one technique in a coherent application. The need to hybridize is easy to understand. Different techniques offer performance that depends on the problem domain. Tasks might require the cooperation of completely different paradigms, such as case-based learning and other forms of symbolic learning with non-symbolic adaptive computing. For these and other reasons, systems that hybridize different machine-learning techniques and eventually expert systems are being proposed.

There is, however, no clear formulation of the problem of hybridization. A number of systems, even some off-the shelf problem-solving software, offer hybridization in the form of a winner-takes-all strategy in which different methods are applied to the solution of a problem, comparisons made, and the best technique selected.

Other systems explore different parts of the problem space with different methodologies, eventually using various methods sequentially. For instance, a genetic algorithm might start to explore an optimization space while the fine optimization is performed by some gradient method, more accurate but more likely to get stuck into local optima. Efforts, both theoretical and practical, are underway to develop hybrid machine-learning paradigms that combine in one single model different techniques that might share some abstract characteristic.

17.7 Clustering, segmentation

Clustering, or segmentation, is the problem of creating a partition of a database so that all members of each set of the partition are similar according to some metric. This problem arises often in finance. One instance is the grouping of stocks or other securities into sets that are maximally homogeneous in function of return or risk parameters. Another instance is the clustering of simulation paths so as to reduce the number of simulations necessary.

The problem of segmentation can be described as follows. Suppose a set A is given, and suppose that for each partition of A into disjoint sets A_j one can define a function $F(A_j)$ that measures some property. One can then build a global function $F(A)$ as the sum of $F(A_j)$:

$$F(A)=\Sigma F(A_j).$$

If the partitioning in sets A_j can be made to correspond to a vector of parameters x, than a function $G(x)$ exists so that

$$F(A)=G(x).$$

It is then possible to define a clustering rule as optimal partitioning, i.e., as the search for the x that maximizes $G(x)$ and, consequently, $F(A)$.

Clustering according to the optimization of set functions finds application in data analysis. It plays a central role in analyzing chaotic systems. One application is to find regions of predictability of time series. Norman Packard, among the founders of the chaos theory and co-founder of The Prediction Company, applied this idea to select partitions that carry the most information content. Dr. Packard later applied this technique to the problem of forecasting currency exchange rates.

There are applications of cluster optimization in other areas, such as setting insurance tariffs. In this application, customers are segmented according to a number of parameters and the optimal tariff segmentation is determined. Another application is the selection of the best areas for business development. In this case, the optimal clustering of factors in function of their location has to be found.

17.8 Adaptive methods in forecasting

Adaptive computational methods are used to determine the relationships that embody the *data-generating process* of a time series so that future values can be computed in function of past and present values. There is an important distinction between stochastic and deterministic forecasting. Ultimately, all forecasts are subject to uncertainty, but the mathematics involved in the two cases is different.

Stochastic forecasting is based on the assumption that the series to be forecast evolves following a certain stochastic model. A stochastic model specifies a probability distribution at every moment, in discrete or continuous time; a data-generating mechanism prescribes the relationship between probability distributions at different moments.

The simplest stochastic models are linear. They include auto-regressive *(*AR) models where any point of the series is a linear combination of previous values plus white noise, and moving-average (MA) models where the generating mechanism is a linear combination of external inputs, and in particular a linear combination of uncorrelated white noise.

Linear models like the AR, MA, and the combined ARMA models have been used for quite a long time. There is a complete methodology for estimating and testing these models, the Box-Jenkins methodology. Useful as a first approximation, linear models suffer from intrinsic limitations when used to describe complex non-linear phenomena.

Stochastic models of increased complexity have been proposed for forecasting financial time series. These express the probability distribution of values at a certain point as a non-linear function of previous values. Among the models proposed are non-linear regression models and the X-ARCH family of models used to describe the clustering of volatilities. Stochastic models can also be described by stochastic differential equations, as, for instance, Ito processes.

Adaptive computational methods are used to determine the parameters that describe models through a process of statistical estimate. This generally involves an optimization process, perhaps using genetic algorithms, to adapt coefficients in function of the sample data. At the end of the process, the system has learned the description of the stochastic mechanism.

A stochastic model of a time series gives an ensemble view of the generating mechanism of the series. It describes not one single "best forecast" trajectory, i.e., one single time series, but a set of trajectories, all compatible with the mathematical constraints that describe the model. Generating one trajectory involves the repeated application of the stochastic mechanism, including the generation of random terms at each step. If one wants, for instance, to compute the possible paths of stock prices that follow an Ito process, he or she must create a suitable discretization of the process that involves, at any step, the generation of a random number. No specific trajectory can be considered the "best" forecast of the process.

The above does not imply that stochastic models cannot be used for forecasting. Stochastic models supply the future probability distribution of values that is the forecast itself. One might use analytical techniques to compute quantities such as the expected values of time series and their standard deviations or higher moments. Alternatively, it is possible to generate a large number of paths and compute the relevant quantities from the set of simulations, as in Monte Carlo methods.

Deterministic forecasting, on the other hand, generates one single path that represents the future evolution of the system. The underlying assumption is the existence of a deterministic data-generating mechanism that can be ascertained with some approximation. This is in line with the tradition of Western science that produces descriptions of physical systems based on differential equations that, with the knowledge of initial and boundary conditions, can be solved forward in time.

In the absence of a theoretical data-generating mechanism, adaptive methods such as neural networks and other approximation schemes have been used. The idea is to create a large number of samples of how sets of successive points are related and to use the samples to train a neural network. One might, for instance, consider a large number of successive $n+1$ points of a financial time series. Of each $(n+1)$-uple, the first n points are the input and the $n+1$ is the output. If a large number of samples are available, a neural network might learn the relationship between inputs and outputs.

The key question is whether a generating function exists and, if it does, how many points need to be considered. The above considers only points that belong to one time series. In practice, it might be necessary to consider many different time series. The principles, however, remain the same.

There is no certainty that a generating function exists or that it is reasonably simple. The series might indeed be random. This means that there is no algorithm shorter than the enumeration of the series necessary to generate it. Alternatively, a generating algorithm might exist but, given the time needed to train a network or any other approximation algorithm, it might be too complex to be practically useful.

Financial time series appear very complex. However, the theory of non-linear dynamic systems has given some hope that this apparent complexity might be reduced to deterministic behavior. The development of non-linear mechanics has in fact shown that non-linear algorithms might be dependent on initial conditions in such a way that even small initial deviations can produce large deviations over time. Weather forecasts show just this type of sensitivity to initial conditions, thereby putting intrinsic limits on the extension of the forecasts. Systems of this type are called chaotic. Systems of even modest complexity can exhibit chaotic behavior.

Trajectories generated by chaotic systems are complex and appear random. An important feature of chaotic systems, however, is that trajectories tend to show statistical regularities and to cluster around geometrical objects called attractors. Attractors might have a dimensionality much smaller than that of the entire system. It can be shown mathematically that if a trajectory is within an attractor of dimensionality d, every point in the time series is a function of only $2d+1$ past values of the series.

If a system follows an attractor of dimensionality d, then the corresponding trajectory can be described by a function of $2d+1$ variables. The theory does not, however, dictate how to ascertain the dimensionality of the eventual attractor. It nevertheless suggests that it is reasonable to plot n-uples of successive values of a time series and to examine if they cluster around attractors. If they do, it is reasonable to forecast with systems of the same dimensionality of the attractor.

With numerous technical variations, the above methodology has been applied to deterministic forecasting. Data analysis techniques have been used to determine the eventual dimensionality of the generating mechanism of a time series and learning algorithms subsequently applied to discover the same generating mechanism.

Deterministic forecasts always present a level of uncertainty. This uncertainty comes from various sources. There are approximations in the learning mechanism, as the generating function is learned through a process of generalization. More fundamentally, even if the data analysis reveals an attractor, this attractor might change its shape or even disappear over time. Attractors are not necessarily stable structures. They might hint at how to determine a data-generating mechanism but, ultimately, they do not solve the forecasting problem; they simply express it differently.

The uncertainty present in deterministic forecasting is the limiting factor for earning excess returns. The forecasting algorithm might effectively reveal potentially profitable dependencies, but the ability to exploit these dependencies is related to the risk involved. Evaluating the performance of a forecasting mechanism implies the evaluation of the uncertainty related to the forecast. Evaluating this uncertainty might, however, be a very difficult task.

17.9 Validation techniques and performance measurement

Machine-learning techniques are adaptive processes that describe data with accuracy that might vary between different domains. Each specific technique offers a generalized description that might be well-adapted to a certain class of phenomena while giving poor results when applied to others. It is, therefore, important to identify techniques that offer an estimate of the performance of any specific technique for a given problem.

Supervised and unsupervised learning present different challenges to performance estimates and validation. In supervised learning, the key point is the ability of the system to generalize from a training set to a full set. This problem is equivalent to the statistical problem of evaluating a probability distribution of a population from a sample.

From a strictly theoretical point of view, the problem of validation cannot be solved, as there is no theoretically sound way to generalize without making generalizing assumptions. Making generalizations from a sample to a much larger universe implies the assumption that the sample is fairly representative and that phenomena can be described by laws that can be learned from the sample.

After making the assumption that generalizations are possible and after building generalizers, there is the technical problem of devising tests and techniques to check if the samples are effectively representative, if they contain enough information to make generalizations, and if the methods used perform well in the given case. As there is normally more than one generalizer, performance evaluation can be used to choose the best generalizer.

A measure of the performance of a classifier is given by the rate and importance of the errors it makes. The true error rate is defined as the ratio between misclassifications and the total number of cases over the entire population.

$$\text{True error rate} = \frac{\text{N of misclassifications}}{\text{N of cases}}.$$

Misclassifications will generally occur not only in the global population but also in the sample set. The error rate over the samples is called the apparent error rate and is defined as follows:

$$\text{Apparent error rate} = \frac{\text{N of misclassified samples}}{\text{N of samples}}.$$

The true error rate is clearly an idealization, as it is the error rate over the entire, potentially infinite, population of cases. Obviously one can set up experiments where the true error rate is measured over the entire population but, in general, only samples are known. It is important to find techniques that allow estimation of the true error rate from the apparent error rate and, eventually, to improve performance.

The error rate is a measure of the performance of a classifier that considers all errors as equally important and simply gives a measure of their frequency. In real-life cases, this might be considered too simplistic. In finance, for example, it is not equally important if falling interest rates are forecasted as rising or vice versa. The size of the error is also important.

To gain a better picture of the error distribution, one needs a misclassification matrix. This is a double-entry table that shows the frequency of each possible misclassification.

In a number of cases, it is possible to give an estimate of the relative importance of misclassifications, associating a cost to each misclassification. As a global measure of the performance of a classifier, one can then take — instead of the error rate — the global cost defined as the sum of each cost E_{ij} times the relative frequency F_{ij} of each type of error:

$$Cost = \Sigma E_{ij} F_{ij}.$$

The benefits of correct classifications can be evaluated in the same way. The difference between gain and cost is a measure of the performance of a classifier. In finance, one must often take into account complex performance measurements. A portfolio manager is interested not in the performance of a specific forecasting algorithm, but in the global risk/return performance of the asset management procedure based on it. Ultimately, performance measurements might be a complex function of errors.

Take, for simplicity, error rates as a measure of performance. During the learning phase, the system is trained on sample cases and its performance is evaluated on the apparent error rate. It would be a serious mistake to take the apparent error rate as a good measure of the true error rate. It can, in fact, be quite the contrary. It is possible to make the apparent error rate very small but the true error rate might be very large. This discrepancy between the apparent and the real error rate might happen because the learning system adapts to fine features characteristic of the samples, but not of the entire population.

If the apparent error rate is not a good measure of performance, how can one measure the performance of a learning system from samples? What is needed is a technique that allows one to measure how a system responds to the essential features of the samples and not to irrelevant details.

An intuitive strategy is to partition the available samples at random into two sets. One, the training set, is used to train the system; the other, the test set, is used to test the performance. In this way, the system is trained on one set of data and tested on another set, avoiding the mistake of estimating performances on the same data set on which the system is trained. It is clearly important that the partitioning used is taken randomly to avoid training and testing on sets affected by spurious correlations.

This technique can be refined in a number of ways. One effective way is resampling. The notion of resampling is simple. The training set is partitioned in many different ways into two complementary sets. For each partition, one set is used for training and the other to test the performance of the generalizer. The same procedure is repeated for every different partition created. A good measure of performance is obtained averaging each individual performance.

One way to partition the training set is called leave-one-out. In this technique, the training set in each partition includes all the training samples but one. The system is then tested on the one left out and the procedure is repeated for each sample. If there are n samples the system is trained on an $(n-1)$ training set and tested on the case left out. The procedure is repeated n times. Each time, the system is trained on different data. Training parameters might, therefore, be different.

It has been demonstrated theoretically and practically that the leave-one-out strategy gives a good performance measure. It is, however, computationally intensive for large samples. Another strategy is to partition the set of samples into k mutually exclusive partitions. Each of the k partitions is used in turn as a test set while the system is trained on the rest of the cases. The procedure is repeated k times and errors are averaged on the k cases.

Bootstrapping is another resampling technique. With bootstrapping, a training set of n elements is created drawn at random, with replacement, from the original set of n samples. Due to the randomness of the choice, some elements in the set of samples will not get chosen to serve as the training set. The system is then tested on these elements. Bootstrapping is particularly indicated when only a small number of samples are available.

The above strategies show how to make the best use of samples in order to achieve a good measure of performance and, eventually, to choose the best generalizer. Resampling techniques were developed in the 1970s to satisfy the needs of statistical analysis and later adopted by the machine-learning community. The principles of resampling are simple and intuitive: to avoid the trap of overspecialization and overoptimistic performance evaluations, do not test performance on the same cases on which the system is trained. Therefore, hold out a number of cases for testing and repeat the procedure with an exhaustive, or at least random, selection of different partitions.

The above techniques apply to measuring the performance of supervised learning. But how is it possible to measure the performance of a system working under unsupervised learning? In unsupervised learning, it is not possible to apply the notion of error and error rates. A system working under unsupervised learning finds a structure autonomously, without making reference to any sample. An important example of unsupervised learning is the clustering of similar cases. At the end of the process, the data set is partitioned into mutually exclusive sets according to a set of rules that the system discovers by itself. In this case, the partitioning cannot be true or false, as each partition will contain a number of cases that will not strictly classify. One measure of the performance of the system could be to evaluate the sharpness of the partitioning, i.e., the level of similarity existing inside each partition.

There is no possibility of defining a performance measure for unsupervised learning as accurately as was possible for supervised learning. Measures must be defined on a case-by-case basis.

References

Advise, L., *Handbook of Genetic Algorithms*, Van Mortared Reined, New York, NY, 1991.

Brahman, L., J. Freedman, R. Olsen and C. Stone, *Classification and Regression Trees*, Wadsworth, Monterey, CA, 1984.

Breeding, J.L. and N.H. Packard, "A Learning Algorithm for Optimal Representations of Experimental Data," *Technical Report CHEERS92-11*, University of Illinois Urbana-Champaign.

Golden, D.E., *Genetic Algorithms in Search, Optimization and Machine Learning*, Addison-Wesley, Reading, MA, 1992.

Goonatilake, S. and P. Treleavan, *Intelligent Systems for Finance and Business*, John Wiley & Sons, London, 1995.

Granger, C.W.J. and P. Newbold, *Forecasting Economic Time Series*, second edition, Academic Press, San Diego, CA, 1986.

Hertz, J., A. Krogh and R. Palmer, *Introduction to the Theory of Neural Computation*, Addison-Wesley, Redwood, CA, 1991.

Hilborn, R.C., *Chaos and Nonlinear Dynamics*, Oxford University Press, New York, NY, 1994.

Holland, J.H., *Adaptation in Natural and Artificial Systems*, second edition, MIT Press, Cambridge, MA, 1992.

Kohonen, T., *Self-Organization and Associative Memory*, Springer-Verlag, Berlin, 1989.

Koza, J.R., *Genetic Programming*, MIT Press, Cambridge, MA, 1993.

Quinlan, J., "Induction of Decision Trees," *Machine Learning*, 1: 81-106, 1986.

Wolpert, D.H., editor, *The Mathematics of Generalization*, Proceedings of the SFI/CNLS Workshop on Formal Approaches to Supervised Learning, Santa Fe Institute, Proceedings Volume XX, 1994.

INDEX

A

ABN-Amro Bank, 16, 18, 132
Adapted stochastic process, 158
Adaptive methods, 12, 66, 67, 99, 102, 111, 119, 121-123, 133, 135. *See also* Computational finance; Finance; Financial applications; Forecasting; Global context
Agent optimality, 1, 169, 197-201
    problem, 2
Agent representation, 200
Agents
    decision-making process, 6, 8, 183
AI. *See* Artificial intelligence
A-J Financial Systems, 45, 110, 139
Algebra/algebras, 150-154, 156-159, 170
Algorithmics, 39, 49, 56, 60, 110, 126, 138
Algorithms, 20, 35, 66, 106, 169. *See also* Forecasting algorithms;
    pricing, 38
    types, 229
Allianz Life Insurance, 124
APAM. *See* Atlantic Portfolio Analytics & Management
Approximation algorithms, 248
Approximators, 66
APT. *See* Arbitrage Pricing Theory
AR. *See* Autoregressive models
Arbitrage, 69, 184. *See also* No arbitrage

B

Y
Yale, 39, 97

Z
Zenios, Stavros, 44, 53, 92, 127
Zerbs, Michael, 39, 49, 60
Zwierzina, Ted, 132